SAVORING
SAVANNAH

Feasts from the Low Country

SAVORING SAVANNAH

Foreword by Nathalie Dupree

Introduction by Martha Giddens Nesbit

Ten Speed Press
Berkeley Toronto

Ten Speed Press
Box 7123
Berkeley, California 94707
www.tenspeed.com

Distributed in Australia by Simon & Schuster Australia, in Canada by Ten Speed Press Canada, in New Zealand by Southern Publishers Group, in South Africa by Real Books, in Southeast Asia by Berkeley Books, and in the United Kingdom and Europe by Airlift Book Company.

 This is a Design Press book. Design Press is a division of the Savannah College of Art and Design.

Printed in Hong Kong
First printing, 2001

1 2 3 4 5 6 7 8 9 10 — 06 05 04 03 02 01

Library of Congress Cataloging-in-Publication Data

Savoring Savannah: feasts from the Low Country / foreword by Nathalie Dupree; introduction by Martha Giddens Nesbit.
    p. cm.
Includes index.
  ISBN 1-58008-252-1
1. Cookery, American—Southern style. 2. Cookery—Georgia—Savannah. 3. Menus. I. Dupree, Nathalie.
  TX715.2.S68 S27   2001
  641.59758'724—dc21   2001002384

Cover and book design by Janice Shay and Winslett Long

Copyediting by Cameron Spencer and Clancy Drake

Research by Elizabeth Hudson-Goff

Principal food photography, black and white photography, and location photography by Daemon Baizan

Photography assistants: Alexis McCraw and Karl Hewig

Additional photography by Deborah Whitlaw:
p. 2, p. 4, p. 6, p. 8, p. 10

Summer Zucchini Salad (p. 16) and Sweet Potato and New Potato Salad (p. 20) recipes are from *Savannah Seasons* by Elizabeth Terry and Alexis Terry. Copyright © 1996 by Elizabeth Terry and Alexis Terry. Used by permission of Doubleday, a division of Random House, Inc.

Stuffed Sirloin of Beef with Wild Mushroom Sauce (p. 130) and Grilled Shrimp Wrapped in Country Bacon with White Bean Cakes and Roasted Red Pepper Vinaigrette (p. 124) recipes are from *A Taste of Heritage: The New African-American Cuisine* by Joe Randall and Toni Tipton-Martin. Copyright © 1998 by Joe Randall and Toni Tipton-Martin. All rights reserved. Reproduced here by permission of the publisher, IDG Books Worldwide, Inc.

Contents

Foreword ⁓

*I*n the heart of the Low Country lies Savannah, Georgia's oldest city, known for her beauty, charm, and gracious hospitality. Savannah is the Hostess City of the South. I have always thought of Savannah as a city who invites you to walk her streets, lounge in her squares, admire her gardens, and enjoy leisurely conversations with her people. The custom of entertaining is a long one in Savannah, and it begins with the welcoming attitude of the city's inhabitants, who display an openness to innovation and who happily embrace the eclectic without fear of losing their own identity. This is a unique Southern city, and the cuisine enjoyed here reflects Savannah's sense of tradition, ethnic influences, and adventurous spirit.

In this book, five of Savannah's top chefs—Elizabeth Terry, Bernard McDonough, George Spriggs, Susan Mason, and Joe Randall—offer their menus and their favorite settings, taking advantage of the variety of cuisine found in Savannah, from crab cakes and tomato sandwiches to potato-crusted sea bass and risotto made with acorn squash and wild rice. *Savoring Savannah: Feasts from the Low Country* draws on the best of what the region has to offer: antebellum hospitality in proud preparations of local produce, seafood, and game.

The evocative photographs of the city and the region set the stage for the dishes. Information abounds throughout the book on the history of Savannah and on the ingredients that make her New Southern cuisine so appealing. The menus for the picnics at Bonaventure Cemetery and at Wormsloe Plantation and the beach party on the informal Tybee Island illustrate the local people's penchant for making even a simple meal a special event. These menus bespeak, too, Savannahians' characteristic appreciation of the outdoors and affection for the romantic atmosphere that attends eating alfresco, surrounded by reminders of the past.

No cookbook from Savannah would be authentic without menus addressing her love for formal dinners. Here, the stately side of Savannah is exhibited in one feast planned around the local tradition of drinking Madeira, and in another that reflects the habit of dining in the residential courtyards typical of the homes in the historic district. Yet another menu both reveals the citizenry's affinity for clubs and acquaints the reader with the

exclusive Married Woman's Card Club, a club that is quintessentially and uniquely Savannahian. The book also includes a Sunday brunch, the after-service meal so much a part of Sunday in the South and relished by the local people as a chance to rest, gossip, and partake of a variety of foods at the leisurely pace that characterizes life in the Low Country.

A recent visit to Savannah rekindled my impression of her as a genteel lady with open arms. These varied feasts offer you the opportunity to experience for yourself why traditional means anything but old-fashioned, staid, static, or conservative. Come, savor Savannah!

—*Nathalie Dupree*

Introduction

Savannah is the jewel of the Low Country—that area made up of marshes and saltwater creeks that teem with shrimp and oysters and provide the rich sandy soil perfect for growing prime vegetables. Her cuisine is legendary—superior ingredients, simply prepared and stunningly presented, graciously offered and politely received, served in the appropriate setting, whether it is historic courtyard, moss-draped cemetery, or beachside sand dune.

Five of the area's most accomplished chefs were asked to offer up their best dishes and suggest settings in which to enjoy them. This book is the result. What you will find in these pages are many of the Low Country's most beloved ingredients—shrimp and oysters, tomatoes, Vidalia onions, sweet potatoes, squash, sesame seeds, blackberries, peaches, pecans, and, of course, grits—presented with new twists guaranteed to please a sophisticated audience of diners.

Savannah is sometimes accused of being stuck in the past. You won't find that to be true of our featured chefs' recipes. These talented culinary artists approached the familiar with a new eye, blending old and new techniques and flavors. They teamed chicken and black-eyed peas, shrimp and fennel, sweet and new potatoes, corn and cucumbers, beef tenderloin and Madeira, pecans and zucchini. They added bacon and Vidalia onions to traditional corn bread, and stuffed figs with goat cheese and herbs. They roasted baby back ribs, rack of venison, and Cornish hens. They pan-fried striped bass, crab cakes, and salmon cakes. They marinated, smoked, and grilled, and they splashed their dishes with vinaigrette.

To round out our offerings, we've included new takes on some traditional Southern dishes that may surprise you. Don't expect rubbery grits and mushy greens: our cooks, inspired by the past but with one foot firmly planted in the future, have created recipes that are anything but ordinary.

—*Martha Giddens Nesbit*

The Chefs

Elizabeth Terry

I am a nurturer, a mother, and I truly believe that food is the energy that we put into our body. I think that something will be beautiful on the plate if you've simply paid attention to nutrition; the colors and textures will happen," says Elizabeth Terry, one of the nation's most acclaimed chefs and a foremother of New Southern cooking.

"Food has long been my passion," admits Elizabeth. "I've always enjoyed poring over old manuscripts of recipes by Southern home cooks." The Southern home cook's practice of keeping a small kitchen garden, where indigenous herbs and vegetables are cultivated so they can be immediately accessible, is an integral feature of Elizabeth on 37th. The restaurant, in a Victorian mansion in the heart of Savannah that Elizabeth and Michael Terry renovated, has become a kind of mecca for people who want to experience Southern cooking at its zenith. Elizabeth Terry takes foods and herbs long savored in Savannah and creates a sophisticated collage of tradition and inventiveness, thus rendering her own signature version of New Southern cuisine.

The bright sun, heat, and humidity make growing herbs and vegetables easy in Savannah. "They don't need cultivation here. And the items we like for soups and salads—garden lettuce, turnips, tiny tomatoes, as well as several herbs—can be literally backdoor-fresh. We have many perennials growing naturally; in fact, downtown gardens feature large hedges of rosemary. I enjoy cooking with herbs not only because they intensify the flavor of food but also because less fat or oil is needed."

The principles and techniques of more than two hundred years of Southern cooking inform every dish on the menu at Elizabeth on 37th, and Elizabeth exhibits an especial appreciation for the stream of ethnic and cultural traditions that influence today's Southern table. Among her awards are the James Beard Best Chef, Southeast Award; Food Arts' Silver Spoon Award; Mobil Travel Guides' Four-Star Award for 1997, 1998, 1999; and *Food & Wine* magazine's Top 25 Restaurants in America, Fine Dining Award.

People in Savannah enjoy life. And Elizabeth Terry enjoys conveying a leisurely fine dining experience with local foods that are the natural treasure of Savannahians.

Bernard McDonough

*B*ernard McDonough began his culinary career with several part-time jobs while attending first Savannah College of Art and Design and later Tulane University in New Orleans. During the summer of 1992, he was given a line cook job at the prestigious 45 South in Savannah under Chef Walter Dasher. By the end of that summer, he had decided not to return to Tulane but to focus his energy solely on cooking.

Today, as the executive chef at the Ford Plantation, the historic home of Henry Ford that is now an exclusive second-home community, Bernie McDonough designs meals and creates dishes that have never before been tasted in Savannah—or, in many instances, anywhere else.

Bernie's philosophy of food reflects his innate passion for high-quality ingredients and his artistic drive to be innovative. He says that his food focuses on the purveyor: "My menus are dictated by what's in season, what's fresh, and what is available to me." For example, he may buy his salmon from the Pacific Coast, one type of goat cheese from California, and tiny hybrid yellow squash from Chef's Garden in Ohio. He likes the notion of eclecticism—bringing big-city dishes found in San Francisco, New York, or Boston and marrying them to traditional regional favorites. Hence, those dining at the Ford Plantation may enjoy a native bird, such as squab, grilled in a Georgia peach teriyaki marinade and served with a ragout of chorizo, black lentils, and potato.

In addition to enjoying finding new ways to pair indigenous foods, Bernie is not afraid to take a risk or to mix a metaphor on the menu, an affectionate nod to the punning humor of his deceased father. That is why the menu may feature "Running with the Deviled Red Lobster Tail" or "Thank Heaven for Little Birds." The menu at the Ford Plantation changes monthly, and members look forward to the variety Bernie's culinary craftiness offers them. For instance, "Something Briny, Something Bubbly" featured a selection of four types of oysters paired with fine champagne.

What would Bernie say is his signature dish? "I don't want a signature dish; if a food I serve becomes my 'signature,' then it is no longer new and different."

What did he have the other night on his day off? "Oh, that's easy. A sweet potato baked in foil and two pounds of peel-and-eat shrimp." Bernie McDonough may have enticed the palate of the South's Hostess City, but the seduction has been mutual.

George Spriggs

George Spriggs's personal style of cooking is best classified as a blend of Southern and Caribbean. He takes traditional Southern food and preparations and adds Caribbean over- and undertones.

"When looking for chefs, I search not only for talent and a knowledge of the basics but also for individuals who are bold and aggressive with their creations and who have a substantial command of the use of herbs, spices, and flavor combinations."

George Spriggs is the co-owner (with George Jackson) and chef of North Beach Grill and of the upscale Georges' of Tybee, both on Tybee Island just east of Savannah. He and Jackson also own Creative Cuisine Catering Services.

Enthralled by the preparation of meals on his grandparents' farm in Florence, South Carolina, where dinner was always an event rather than a meal, George developed an early taste for what is good and authentic about Southern cooking. He was able to see the whole journey of his family's food—"from the garden, field, or holding pen to its final edible state."

George's experience in the food service industry started on the other end of the restaurant, however—in the front, where he worked as a waiter. After five years in this role, the opportunity arose for him and Jackson to open a beachside concession stand. When a regular patron asked them to prepare a full meal for a party, George realized that he had found his calling. Soon after, North Beach Grill was established. At North Beach Grill, the surf provides the mood, and diners in flip-flops munch on jerk chicken or Key lime pie and drink wine from plastic cups.

Georges' of Tybee is the Georges latest culinary enterprise. It is a handsome restaurant where diners enjoy their chardonnay in delicate glasses and savor gourmet combinations of seafood, fowl, meats, and the freshest vegetables in the quiet manner of fine dining. Georges' of Tybee has received rave reviews from regional and national publications, and it is consistently booked solid.

Susan Mason

Susan Mason's family home in Dothan, Alabama, may have been the smallest house on the block, but it was bursting with people who were welcome to enjoy the hospitality of home cooking. "Our family always said 'I love you' with food," she says. "You never knew who would be there for dinner."

Every year Susan and her mother, two aunts, and two sisters (with an occasional sister-in-law) would travel to Europe, rent a van, and ride throughout the western nations discussing food and different ways to prepare it. "We associated people and events with the food that the people made or that was served at the event. Somehow our lives have always revolved around food."

Susan was acting as cochair of a charity ball when the idea of having a catering business occurred to her. Within three years she and her partner were catering the governor's daughter's wedding in the Governor's Mansion in Columbia, South Carolina. He had a great kitchen staff, she says; there was one chef and a cooking staff of local prisoners only too willing to work and to plesase.

Today, after fifteen years as the most in-demand caterer in Savannah, Susan asserts that her philosophy on her business and success is simple: "I offer Savannahians what they like and want." She also credits her own love of people and the dedication and pride that her staff demonstrate in their work. "I wave the baton; they make the music," she says. "I also was told to know my limitations; and I told myself I have no limitations." Her business is a stressful one, in that she expects perfection from herself. The biggest challenge she sees in Savannah is, quite understandably, the heat. It's not easy to keep 1,500 crab cakes cold for a dinner that is being served in a picnic area fifty miles north of the home city.

Some of her secrets? "I use the best ingredients—I don't cut corners. I always use the highest quality cuts of meat, the best produce, and the freshest seafood—which is one of the advantages of being in Savannah. And I always overbuy; I don't ever want to run short of food."

Presentation is inherently important, and Susan is known in Savannah for her elegant style. Susan appreciates a skill that is innate for many girls brought up in the traditional South: "We enjoy using our inherited china, our best crystal. Food that looks good and is garnished well tastes good too."

So what does Susan Mason make for herself on days when she is not catering a wedding for one thousand or a tea party for two hundred? "Salmon steak with risotto. And I love to play with sauces—it's fun to create new ones."

Joe Randall

*A*s a boy, Joe Randall enjoyed accompanying his mother and grandmother to the 135-year-old farmers' market near his home, where he came to appreciate the freshest produce, a variety of cheeses, and all cuts of meat.

"My uncle, restaurateur Richard Ross, first gave me a tease for the culinary career. It later became a joy to develop the menus for restaurants built upon African-American cuisine and to be totally committed to the authenticity of food," says "Chef Joe," a thirty-year veteran of the hospitality and food service industry.

Chef Randall believes that the food of Savannah is truly the food of the South, offering the marriage of Gullah-Geechee ("rice eater") tradition with the abundance of seafood and traditional Southern seasonings. "Well-seasoned food is not overpowered by spice," declares Joe. The basic Southern spices in any pantry, he says, are "salt, pepper, and cayenne; you need just enough cayenne to say 'hello.'"

Here in Savannah, attests Joe, is the opportunity to put a new twist on old things and make dishes of the past contemporary. His guiding philosophy is to cook from one's roots. Pork is a major flavor in many of Chef Randall's recipes, and it appears in several incarnations—salt pork, ham hocks, and slab bacon. "I cook more than collard greens and fried chicken. When Southern chefs do their job right, they lift Southern food to its rightful place among the top cuisines of the world."

Joe Randall has received many awards, among them the Distinguished Service Award from the National Institute for the Food Service Industry, and gold, silver, and bronze medals in culinary competitions. In 1993, he founded A Taste of Heritage Foundation, a nonprofit organization that addresses career-related issues having impact on African Americans in the hospitality industry. In 1995, the Culinary Institute of America's Black Culinary Alumni awarded him the Lifetime Leadership Award for his efforts to advance the culinary contribution of African-American chefs. In 1998, he coauthored *A Taste of Heritage: The New African-American Cuisine*, a cookbook melding older traditions with new directions. Today he heads a thriving catering business and enjoys teaching others the rewards of cooking at Chef Joe Randall's Cooking School in Savannah, where eager culinary students learn the significance of Chef Joe's motto: "Put some South in your mouth."

Chef Elizabeth Terry's

Garden Anniversary
Luncheon

Serves 6

❧

"I like to put everything on the table to serve—even the dessert. I love to watch my guests' anticipation for that beautiful double cherry pie. Serve the garden party dishes on platters or in large bowls with serving spoons. I collect platters, bowls, and serving pieces on family trips. Nothing 'matches,' but they each evoke wonderful memories from the occasion of their acquisition."

❧

Shrimp and Fennel Salad

Summer Zucchini Salad

Sesame Chicken and Black-Eyed Pea Salad

Corn and Cucumber Relish

Sweet Potato and New Potato Salad

Sweet Potato Brioche

Double Cherry Pie

❧

She spread a table for us, brilliant with white linen, and china, and silver, and entertained us with tea and bread and butter, potatoes at my desire, eggs, and other good things. No, it would not have been more possible for a meal spread by fairy hands to have been more delicate or finely flavored. . . . Savannah might be called the city of the gushing springs: there can not be, in the whole world, a more beautiful city than Savannah!

—FREDRIKA BREMER (1853)

Elizabeth and Michael Terry bought a six-thousand-square-foot, turn-of-the-century Southern mansion on 37th Street in Savannah in 1980. They renovated the downstairs into an elegant restaurant and moved the family— including now-grown daughters Alexis and Celeste—happily into the upstairs quarters. Almost immediately, the restaurant drew locals and tourists wanting to experience fine dining reminiscent of Southern eighteenth- and nineteenth-century dinner parties. It wasn't long before Elizabeth was discovered by food writers. She has been featured in just about every food magazine in this country and in a number of international ones, as well as in dozens of newspapers, and is the recipient of a number of the nation's most prestigious food awards.

Elizabeth cooks seasonally, presenting the best of whatever is available in fresh and interesting ways and serving it in an elegant setting, with a knowledgeable wait staff who epitomize Southern hospitality. Critical to her style of cooking are fresh herbs, typically snipped from the lush garden that she lovingly designed, planted, and tends. Today the herb garden literally envelops the restaurant, and it attracts gardeners as well as diners. Elizabeth uses thyme, rosemary, and sage—especially pineapple sage—in her dishes. Another back-of-the-house garden keeps the kitchen staff supplied with unusual vegetables, lettuces, and edible flowers. Such a savory setting lends itself to any outdoor celebratory meal—a special birthday, an anniversary, or simply the first day of spring.

Most herbs in Elizabeth's garden can be traced to ancient Mediterranean gardens. There is evidence that basil, marjoram, oregano, mint, rosemary, thyme, dill, and parsley, among many others, were enjoyed by our Greek and Roman forebears for culinary and medicinal purposes. During the Middle Ages, "salats" were constructed of a variety of fresh green herbs, garlic, leeks, onions, and vinegar—a strong "salat palette" indeed!

Shrimp and Fennel Salad

This dish pairs the ever popular Low Country shrimp with fresh fennel—a delightful combination of delicate flavors and contrasting textures.

Salad

1 teaspoon pickling spices, tied in cheesecloth
1¹/₂ pounds jumbo shrimp (21 to 25 count), peeled, deveined, and tails removed
1 tablespoon dark sesame oil
1 tablespoon extra virgin olive oil
2 fennel bulbs, very thinly sliced
¹/₂ red onion or Vidalia onion, very thinly sliced
1¹/₂ teaspoons coriander seeds, toasted (*page 18*)

Dressing

1 clove garlic, minced
2 shallots, minced
1 tablespoon balsamic vinegar
2 tablespoons dark sesame oil
Salt
Freshly ground black pepper

To prepare the salad, put the pickling spices in a large pot with 3 quarts of water and bring to a boil. Add the shrimp and cook for 2 to 3 minutes, until pink. Remove the shrimp with a slotted spoon and set aside.

In a large skillet, heat the sesame and olive oils over medium-high heat. Add the fennel and sauté for 10 to 12 minutes, until crisp-tender. Remove from the heat. Add the onion and coriander seeds, and set aside to cool.

To prepare the dressing, whisk all ingredients together in a small bowl.

To serve, arrange the fennel-onion mixture on a large platter, top with the shrimp, and drizzle with the dressing.

Summer Zucchini Salad

Although zucchini is not native to Savannah, summer squash, the suggested substitute, certainly is. Georgia pecans add crunch and their own unmistakable Low Country flavor.

$^1/_4$ cup pecans

8 zucchini or summer squash, scrubbed well

$^1/_4$ cup extra virgin olive oil

4 cloves garlic, minced

$^1/_4$ cup fresh basil leaves, julienned

2 tablespoons fresh mint leaves, julienned

$^1/_2$ teaspoon salt

To toast the pecans, preheat the oven to 325°. Spread the pecans on an ungreased baking sheet and bake for 5 minutes until lightly browned. Check and stir them often to prevent burning and toughening. Remove from the oven and allow to cool, then mince.

Trim the ends of the zucchini and halve them lengthwise. With a spoon, scrape out the seeds, leaving $^1/_4$ inch of flesh around the edges. Slice the zucchini into $^1/_4$-inch-thick strips, then slice the strips into matchsticks. You should have about 4 cups of zucchini. In a large skillet, heat the oil over medium-high heat. Add the zucchini and garlic, and sauté until the zucchini is crisp-tender, about 3 minutes. Remove the zucchini from the pan and spread on a plate to cool. When cool, put it in a bowl and toss with the basil, mint, salt, and pecans. Serve at room temperature.

A wide variety of vegetables were enjoyed by Southerners long before their Northern neighbors caught on. The old City Market in Savannah overflowed with vegetables such as beets, okra, squashes, beans, turnips, sweet potatoes, and eggplant as early as 1800.

Sesame Chicken and Black-Eyed Pea Salad

This recipe marries the oil and crunch of the sesame seed—so integral to Low Country cuisine—with the dry taste of the traditional black-eyed pea—such a staple in the South. The addition of mint and parsley brightens the flavors of both.

Dressing

5 teaspoons honey
2 tablespoons coarse-grain mustard
2 teaspoons soy sauce
$^1/_4$ cup apple cider vinegar
$^1/_4$ cup extra virgin olive oil
$^1/_4$ cup dark sesame oil

Salad

$^1/_4$ cup sesame seeds
2 tablespoons dark sesame oil
1 teaspoon apple cider vinegar
$^1/_4$ cup fresh mint leaves, minced
1 teaspoon freshly cracked black pepper
5 boneless, skinless chicken breast halves
2 teaspoons salt
$^3/_4$ cup water chestnuts or fresh celeriac, minced
5 whole scallions, minced
$^1/_2$ cup flat-leaf parsley, minced
$^1/_2$ cup golden raisins, minced
5 cups mixed salad greens
1 (15-ounce) can black-eyed peas, drained and rinsed

To prepare the dressing, bring all the ingredients to room temperature. In a large bowl, whisk together the honey, mustard, soy sauce, and vinegar. While whisking constantly, slowly add the oils. When the dressing thickens slightly, set aside.

To prepare the salad, first toast the sesame seeds: place them in a dry skillet over medium heat. Cook for about 4 minutes, or just until the seeds begin to release a hint of fragrance, stirring or shaking often to prevent burning. (This method may also be used to toast coriander, fennel, and cumin seeds.)

In a shallow, nonreactive dish, whisk together the oil, vinegar, mint, and pepper. Coat both sides of each chicken breast with this marinade, cover, and refrigerate for at least 30 minutes and up to 6 hours.

Black-eyed peas, which are African in origin, have been a staple food in the South for three hundred years. A popular dish on New Year's Day, black-eyed peas are associated with good luck.

Heat a large skillet over medium heat. Add the chicken breasts and sauté, turning once, until lightly browned and cooked through, about 3 minutes per side. Remove from the heat. When cool enough to handle, dice the chicken. Transfer to a bowl and toss with the pan juices, salt, water chestnuts, scallions, parsley, and raisins. Refrigerate for at least 2 hours and no longer than 12.

Just before serving, arrange the greens on a large platter. Toss the dressing with the chicken, then spoon it on top of the greens. Garnish with the black-eyed peas and toasted sesame seeds.

Corn and Cucumber Relish

Both corn and cucumbers abound locally. The jalapeño provides heat at the back of the mouth, not on the tip of the tongue, so that it enhances rather than interferes with the taste of this relish.

2 ears of corn, shucked and trimmed
2 small cucumbers, peeled, seeded, and finely diced
I large red bell pepper, seeded, deribbed, and finely diced
I small stalk celery, finely diced
I small onion, finely chopped
I large clove garlic, finely diced
I jalapeño chile, seeded, cored, and minced
3 tablespoons freshly squeezed lime juice
$^1/_2$ teaspoon ground cumin
$^1/_2$ teaspoon salt
$^1/_3$ cup cilantro, chopped

Cook the corn in boiling salted water for 4 minutes. Drain, and rinse under cold water. Scrape the corn kernels from the cob. In a bowl, combine the corn with the remaining ingredients. Cover and refrigerate for at least 1 hour. Serve chilled in a large bowl.

Sweet Potato and New Potato Salad

The seasoning of this unique side dish offers a savory approach to an outdoor luncheon favorite, rather than the tart one supplied by the more usual white distilled vinegar. The bright green of the spinach highlights the fresh taste provided by the fruit, so restorative on a hot Georgia day.

Dressing
2 shallots, minced
8 cloves garlic, minced
1 tablespoon raspberry vinegar
1 tablespoon Dijon mustard
1 cup fresh spinach, minced
1/4 cup fresh basil leaves, minced
1/4 cup fresh mint leaves, minced
1/4 cup vegetable oil
2 tablespoons extra virgin olive oil
1 teaspoon salt
1 tablespoon hot water

Salad
2 sweet potatoes, peeled and diced into 1/4-inch pieces
10 (1 1/2-inch) new red potatoes, sliced
1 teaspoon freshly cracked pepper
1 bunch watercress, stemmed
1/2 cup halved green or red seedless grapes
1/2 pint fresh raspberries

To prepare the dressing, combine the shallots, garlic, vinegar, mustard, spinach, basil, and mint in the bowl of a food processor. With the motor running on low speed, slowly add the oils, then the salt and hot water. The dressing will be bright green and should have the consistency of a sauce.

To prepare the salad, bring water to a boil in two separate pots and boil the sweet potatoes and the new potatoes separately until fork-tender, about 10 minutes. Drain the potatoes and combine them in a bowl. Toss with 1/4 cup of the dressing and the pepper, cover, and refrigerate for at least 2 hours and no longer than 12. Before serving, remove the potatoes from the refrigerator and let them come to room temperature. To serve, place a bed of watercress on each salad plate, top with the potatoes, and drizzle with the rest of the dressing. Sprinkle the grapes and raspberries on top. Serve at room temperature.

Sweet Potato Brioche

Toasting brings out the flavor of this rich, buttery bread—great for making ahead.

1 tablespoon active dry yeast
1 tablespoon sugar
¹/₄ cup warm water
¹/₂ cup melted unsalted butter, at room temperature
¹/₂ teaspoon salt
1 teaspoon freshly cracked black pepper
2 cups all-purpose flour
¹/₃ cup cooked sweet potato, peeled and diced into ¹/₄-inch pieces
2 eggs

Butter a large bowl and a 9 by 5-inch loaf pan. In the bowl of a stand mixer, combine the yeast, sugar, and water, and mix on low speed. Allow the mixture to sit for 10 minutes, until bubbles form. Add the melted butter, salt, pepper, flour, sweet potato, and eggs, and mix with a dough hook on low speed until the mixture is smooth, 5 to 10 minutes. Put the dough in the prepared bowl, cover with a towel, and allow to rise until doubled in size, 1 to 1¹/₂ hours but no longer.

Shape the dough into a loaf and place it in the prepared pan. Cover with the towel and allow to rise for 1 hour, no longer.

Preheat the oven to 400°. Bake for 25 minutes, until golden. Remove from the oven, invert onto a rack, and allow to cool before slicing.

"To test an oven for bread, pastry and other cereals, a bit of paper may be placed in it and if it turns a dark brown in 5 minutes, the heat is just right. An oven intended to be moderately hot, for cakes, delicate puddings, etc., should burn a bit of white paper yellow in 5 minutes."

—Favorite Recipes from Savannah Homes (1904)

Double Cherry Pie

Neither of these cherries is indigenous to coastal Georgia, but what meal would be complete in the Hostess City of the South without some welcome visitors?

Pie Crust (for a two-crust pie)

1 1/2 cups all-purpose flour
1/2 teaspoon ground cinnamon
2 tablespoons sugar
1/2 cup unsalted butter, chilled and cut into 1/2-inch cubes
4 tablespoons very cold water

2 3/4 cups Bing cherries, pitted and halved
2 3/4 cups Rainier cherries, pitted and halved
3 tablespoons cornstarch
3 tablespoons quick-cooking tapioca
1 cup sugar
1/2 teaspoon ground cinnamon
1 tablespoon freshly squeezed lemon juice

To prepare the pie crust, butter a 9-inch pie pan and set it aside. In the bowl of a food processor (or with your fingertips), combine the flour, cinnamon, sugar, and butter. Pulse to combine until the mixture resembles coarse meal. With the motor running, slowly pour in the water. Pulse just a few seconds until the mixture begins to form a mass. Remove from the processor and shape into a flat disk. Wrap in plastic wrap and and refrigerate for 30 minutes.

Divide the dough into 2 equal parts. On a floured surface, roll one part of the dough into a circle 1/8 inch thick and about 11 inches in diameter. Transfer to the prepared pie pan, allowing the extra dough to hang over the edge of the pan. Refrigerate until ready to use, at least 30 minutes.

Roll the second part of the dough out on a floured surface into a 1/8-inch-thick, 10-inch square. Cut the square into 8 equal strips about 1 inch wide. Refrigerate until ready to use, at least 30 minutes.

Preheat the oven to 375°. To prepare the filling, combine the cherries, cornstarch, tapioca, sugar, cinnamon, and lemon juice in a large bowl. Spoon into the chilled pie shell. Moisten the edge of the crust with cold water. Lay 4 dough strips evenly across the top of the pie about 1/2 inch apart. Working perpendicularly, weave the fifth strip over and under the others. Repeat with the other strips, alternating the pattern to achieve a basket-weave design. Trim the crust around the edge of the pie to about 1 inch larger than the pan and fold up over the lattice strips and crimp together to seal. Bake on the middle rack for 50 minutes, until the fruit bubbles and the crust is brown. Put a sheet pan on the shelf below the pie to catch any drippings. Allow to cool before slicing.

Chef Elizabeth Terry's
Formal Madeira Dinner

Serves 6

Wines in italics are suggested accompaniments to each dish.

❧

"Requisition your children to serve your formal dinner. I worked out an exchange: Celeste and Alexis served dinner for me, and I served homemade pizza to their friends."

❧

Cream of Butternut Squash Soup
Cossart Gordon Rainwater Medium Dry

Herbs and Greens with Madeira Vinaigrette
15-year Malmsey Blandy's

Beef Tenderloin with Madeira Sauce

Oven-Roasted New Potatoes (page 133)
5-year Malmsey Cossart Gordon

Sweet Potato Pies
1966 Bual Leacock

❧

The Trustees, receiving frequent information from the colony of the pernicious effects of drinking rum and other spirituous liquors, by not only creating disorders amongst the Indians, but also of destroying many of the English, and throwing the people into various distempers, prepared an act, entitled, 'Act to Prevent the Importation and Use of Rum and Brandies in the Province of Georgia, or any kind of spirits or strong waters whatsoever.' At the same time they endeavored to supply the stores with strong beer from England, molasses for brewing beer, and with Madeira wines, which the people might purchase at reasonable rates, and which would be more refreshing and wholesome for them.

—GEORGIA HISTORICAL SOCIETY (January 1843)

At his death in 1832, Alexander Telfair's wine cellar contained 714 bottles and 18 gallons of wine, in addition to 152 empty bottles. Most of those wines were Madeiras, the favorite wine of Savannah's most distinguished citizens. Although early in Savannah's history Madeira vines were brought to the city from the island of Madeira, they never took root. Residents discovered, however, that the wine seemed to improve in flavor during its passage from Madeira to Savannah, and it further improved with storage in the mild Savannah climate.

No wonder Madeira parties became popular in the years leading up to the Civil War! Guests were invited in at 5 P.M. for an hour or so of tasting that typically included a half-dozen Madeiras and appropriate accompaniments.

Madeira was so enjoyed in early Savannah that aficionados created a group, the Madeira Society, that is extant today. This rather mysterious group, which still consists only of men, upholds the bylaws of the group that first met in the mid-eighteenth century, meeting once a month for Madeira tastings, dinner, and general discussion. Madeira appreciation is an art unto itself, and the wines' complex bouquets inspire deep respect.

Cream of Butternut Squash Soup

This brightly colored introduction to the meal combines ginger and orange juice. I like the contrasting flavors of the Madeira being sipped and the cooked Madeira in the pear purée.

Chicken Stock
Makes 6 cups

2 pounds chicken pieces, well rinsed
7 cups water
1 large onion, chopped into $\frac{1}{2}$-inch pieces
2 carrots, cut into $\frac{1}{2}$-inch slices
1 stalk celery, chopped into $\frac{1}{2}$-inch pieces
3 whole black peppercorns
1 bay leaf

1 butternut squash, peeled, seeded, and chopped
1 sweet potato, peeled and chopped
1 large Vidalia or Spanish onion, chopped
2 cloves garlic, chopped
1 ($\frac{1}{2}$-inch by 1-inch) piece fresh ginger, peeled and chopped
$\frac{1}{2}$ cup heavy cream
$\frac{1}{4}$ cup freshly squeezed orange juice
1 tablespoon freshly squeezed lemon juice
1 teaspoon hot sauce
Salt
1 pear, peeled, seeded, and chopped
$\frac{1}{2}$ cup Madeira
Society garlic blossoms or chive blossoms, for garnish (optional)

To prepare the stock, put the chicken and water in a large pot over high heat and bring almost to a boil. Decrease the heat to medium-low and simmer gently for 10 minutes. Skim off any foam or impurities from the top. Add the onion, carrots, celery, peppercorns, and bay leaf and simmer uncovered until the chicken is cooked, about 40 minutes. Remove the chicken. Strain the stock through a fine-meshed sieve into a clean pot. Allow to cool completely, uncovered, then refrigerate. Fat can be skimmed from the top before using.

To prepare the soup, combine the stock, squash, sweet potato, onion, garlic, and ginger in a large soup pot over medium heat. Bring to a boil, then decrease the heat

to low. Cover and simmer until the vegetables are very soft, about 40 minutes. Purée in batches in a blender until smooth, then return to the pot and whisk in the cream, orange juice, lemon juice, and hot sauce. Before serving, rewarm over medium-high heat but do not allow to boil. Season to taste with salt.

In a small saucepan over medium heat, combine the pear and Madeira and cook for 10 to 15 minutes until soft. In a blender on low speed, purée the pear and Madeira together until smooth.

Ladle the soup into individual bowls and drizzle the pear-Madeira purée over each just before serving. Garnish with garlic blossoms.

Herbs and Greens with Madeira Vinaigrette

Madeira is particularly great for cooking; it will keep for up to three years and works as well in a cream sauce as it does in a vinaigrette.

6 ounces mixed baby greens
1 cup flat-leaf parsley leaves
1 cup mixed herb leaves, including tarragon, mint, basil, and fennel tops
2 tablespoons Malmsey Madeira
1 tablespoon rice wine vinegar
2 tablespoons extra virgin olive oil
$^1/_2$ teaspoon salt
$^1/_2$ teaspoon freshly ground black pepper
$^1/_4$ cup dried cranberries, chopped, for garnish (optional)

Combine the greens, parsley, and herbs in a bowl and set aside. In a large bowl, whisk together the Madeira and vinegar. Gradually whisk in the oil. Tilt the bowl so that the dressing covers the sides and bottom. Add the greens and herbs, season with the salt and pepper, and lightly toss to coat the leaves. Divide among 6 plates, garnish with the cranberries, and serve.

Beef Tenderloin with Madeira Sauce

This classic peppered beef dish, with the added warmth of Madeira, is especially welcome on a chilly winter evening. The combination of the three peppers and the coriander lends a most subtle flavor to a traditional favorite. Oven-roasted new potatoes are a nice accompaniment.

3 tablespoons coarsely ground mixed black, white, and green pepper
1 tablespoon ground coriander
1 tablespoon salt
$2^1/_2$ pounds beef tenderloin, in one piece, trimmed
2 tablespoons extra virgin olive oil
1 cup heavy cream
1 cup Madeira

Preheat the oven to 375°. In a small bowl, mix together the pepper, coriander, and salt. Press the spice mixture onto all sides of the tenderloin. Heat the oil over high

heat in a large cast-iron skillet. When the oil is sizzling hot, quickly sear all sides of the tenderloin in the skillet until browned; this should take about 5 minutes. Transfer the skillet to the oven and roast the meat for 30 minutes until medium-rare. Remove the meat from the oven and transfer to a cutting board. Let rest at room temperature for 5 minutes to allow the juices to return to the center of the roast.

While the meat rests, set the skillet with the pan drippings over medium-high heat. Add the cream and Madeira and stir to loosen any browned bits, incorporating them into the cream. Bring to a rolling boil for 5 minutes, until thick and creamy. Taste and adjust seasoning. Slice the tenderloin into thick slices. Divide the meat among 6 plates, top with a drizzle of cream sauce, and pass any extra sauce.

The practice of cooking meats until well done was not common until the mid- to late nineteenth century, with the advent of the iron kitchen range. Prior to this time, Southern cooks continued the tradition of their English forebears of roasting meats over a fire, on a spit turned by a jack. It was believed that meats roasted rare were the best tasting and most healthful.

Sweet Potato Pies

This recipe is my new favorite dessert. It is the creation of my long-time pastry chef, Stephanie Hall-Jones. It can be served warm or at room temperature and is best served with whipped cream or a scoop of ice cream.

Caramel Crumb Crust

²/₃ cup all-purpose flour

¹/₃ cup firmly packed brown sugar

¹/₃ cup unsalted butter

Filling

3 or 4 large sweet potatoes, peeled and chopped into ¹/₂-inch cubes (about 4 cups)

2¹/₄ cups granulated sugar

¹/₂ cup unsalted butter

1 tablespoon vanilla extract

¹/₄ cup all-purpose flour

¹/₄ cup milk

3 eggs

1 teaspoon ground nutmeg

1 teaspoon ground cinnamon

Whipped cream, for serving

Orange Sauce

Makes 2 cups

4 cups freshly squeezed orange juice

³/₄ cup sugar

3 teaspoons arrowroot, dissolved in 2 teaspoons water

1 tablespoon freshly squeezed lemon juice

1 tablespoon grated lemon zest

2 teaspoons grated orange zest

Candied orange zest, for garnish

To prepare the crust, combine all the ingredients in a food processor and process until the butter is incorporated and the mixture resembles coarse meal. Spray 6 (9-ounce) custard cups with nonstick spray. Divide the crumbs equally among the cups.

Preheat the oven to 325°. To prepare the filling, put the sweet potatoes in a pot with enough water to cover. Boil until soft, 5 to 10 minutes, then drain. Put the sweet potatoes in a large bowl and add the rest of the filling ingredients. Mash and mix until they are thoroughly combined.

Divide the filling evenly among the custard cups. Bake for 25 to 30 minutes, until set. The pies can be served in the custard cups or turned onto plates—carefully. Surround with whipped cream.

To make the sauce, reduce the orange juice to 2 cups in a large, nonreactive saucepan over medium heat. Add the sugar and dissolved arrowroot to the reduced orange juice. Simmer for 1 minute, until the mixture is very slightly thickened. Allow to cool. Add the lemon juice and lemon and orange zests. The sauce will be thin. Cover and refrigerate until needed. This sauce can be refrigerated for at least 3 weeks. To serve, gently drizzle the sauce over the whipped cream and decorate with candied orange zest.

Chef Bernard McDonough's

Picnic at Bonaventure Cemetery

Serves 6

❦

"With this menu, I like to just spread the whole thing out and let people pick out what they want. The tapenade and spinach, crab, and artichoke dip are spread on any good, crusty French bread. I like to just pick up the figs and pop them in my mouth."

❦

Kalamata Olive Tapenade

Smoked Shrimp and Melon Gazpacho

Marinated Vine-Ripened Tomatoes

Spinach, Crab, and Artichoke Dip

Grilled Figs with Prosciutto and Goat Cheese

WD's Spicy Smoky Corn Bread

Strawberry Mint Sweet Tea

Walter Dasher's Coconut Fudge Brownies

❦

I gazed awe-stricken as one new-arrived from another world. Bonaventure is called a graveyard, a town of the dead, but the few graves are powerless in such a depth of life. The rippling of living waters, the song of birds, the joyful confidence of flowers, the calm, undisturbable grandeur of the oaks, mark this place of graves as one of the Lord's most favored abodes of life and light.

—JOHN MUIR (early 1900s)

Bonaventure is the most beautiful cemetery in America. At least that is the way John Berendt described it in *Midnight in the Garden of Good and Evil*, his blockbuster 1994 novel, which featured one of the most memorable statues in the cemetery on the cover. Since *Midnight*, interest in Bonaventure has caused an influx of visitors who want to see for themselves the live oaks dripping moss, the blooming spring azaleas, and the waterfowl searching for supper in the Wilmington River visible from the high bluff. Those who have the time and inclination also like to walk from family plot to family plot in search of interesting monuments and familiar names, such as colonist Nobel Jones, Governor Edward Telfair, poet Conrad Aiken, and lyricist Johnny Mercer.

Once a thriving plantation run by Colonel John Mulryne and his son-in-law, Josiah Tatnall, the property was purchased by the city of Savannah in 1907, and the original plantation name, Bonaventure—meaning "good fortune"—was restored. Today the cemetery's 160 acres have vacancies, though plot reservations are coveted. "One of my friends (a prominent Savannah businessman) bought a plot at Bonaventure for each of his closest friends, including me," caterer Susan Mason reports. "Now *that* was a present!"

Chef Bernard McDonough of the Ford Plantation was eager to stage a party on such romantic turf. Although the midnight martini is off-limits (the cemetery is open to the public from 8 A.M. to 5 P.M. daily), one might choose a spot on the high bluff overlooking the river for dining. Guests are asked not to litter; to be kind to the aging, fragile roads and monuments; and, of course, never to inter-fere with a funeral.

Kalamata Olive Tapenade

A tapenade is a great picnic dish—it's easy and portable. Tapenade is best spread on crusty French bread slices.

2 cups drained pitted kalamata olives
$1/2$ cup freshly grated Parmesan cheese
1 small bunch fresh basil, chopped
2 teaspoons fresh rosemary, chopped
2 teaspoons fresh thyme, chopped
$1/4$ cup extra virgin olive oil
Freshly cracked black pepper

Combine the olives, cheese, basil, rosemary, and thyme in a food processor and process until smooth. With the motor still running, slowly drizzle in the oil. Season to taste with pepper. Cover and refrigerate until serving.

Smoked Shrimp and Melon Gazpacho

Cold soup is always refreshing; this one is made sweet by the addition of fruit. Although many commercial smokers are available, I find the classic side firebox, or indirect heat, the most predictable. Simply grilling the shrimp will work but will sacrifice flavor.

$^3/_4$ pound extra-large fresh shrimp (26 to 30 count), peeled and deveined
2 large vine-ripened tomatoes
2 tablespoons extra virgin olive oil
2 tablespoons red wine vinegar
$^3/_4$ cup chopped cantaloupe, honeydew, or watermelon (about $^1/_4$ of a small melon)
$^1/_2$ large cucumber, chopped
$^1/_4$ Vidalia onion, chopped
$^1/_2$ red, green, or yellow bell pepper, seeded, deribbed, and chopped
24 fresh chives, chopped
Pinch of ground cumin
Pinch of ground coriander
Salt
Freshly cracked black pepper
Hot sauce (optional)

Preheat the oven to 350°. Smoke the shrimp over hickory, mesquite, or oak according to the smoker manufacturer's directions, until shrimp are firm and opaque. Set aside 12 of the shrimp for garnish.

Put the tomatoes in a roasting pan and roast for 15 to 20 minutes, until soft and golden brown and the skin begins to crack. Allow to cool, then transfer to a blender. Purée on high speed until smooth, then slowly pour in the oil and vinegar while the blender is still on high speed. Roughly chop the shrimp and combine it with the melon, cucumber, onion, bell pepper, and chives in a large bowl. Stir in the puréed tomato mixture, cumin, coriander, and salt, pepper, and hot sauce to taste. Cover and refrigerate no longer than 2 to 4 hours before serving in individual bowls. Garnish each serving with 2 of the reserved whole shrimp.

Marinated Vine-Ripened Tomatoes

This is a simple make-ahead Southern standard with an Italian twist.

4 vine-ripened tomatoes, coarsely chopped
2 cloves garlic, minced
1/2 cup fresh tarragon, chopped
2 tablespoons balsamic vinegar
2 tablespoons extra virgin olive oil
Salt
Freshly cracked black pepper

Combine all the ingredients in a bowl. Refrigerate for at least 8 hours before serving. Serve as a side dish with a slotted spoon.

Spinach, Crab, and Artichoke Dip

This is a classic American dish with the addition of the local flavor provided by the abundance of blue crabs in the Low Country. The nutmeg brings out the flavor of the spinach. Serve with crusty French bread.

1/4 pound crabmeat, preferably claw
1/2 pound jumbo lump blue crab meat
1 tablespoon unsalted butter
1 cup spinach, chopped
1/4 cup cooked artichoke hearts, thinly sliced
2 tablespoons chopped roasted red bell pepper (*page 127*)
1/4 cup fresh chèvre, crumbled
1/4 cup cream cheese, at room temperature
Nutmeg
Salt
Freshly ground black pepper

Check all the crabmeat thoroughly for shells. In a sauté pan, melt the butter over medium-high heat. Add the spinach and sauté for about 2 minutes, until very tender and bright green. In a bowl, combine the claw meat, spinach, artichoke hearts, bell pepper, chèvre, and cream cheese and season to taste with nutmeg, salt, and pepper. After mixing well, gently fold in the lump crabmeat. Cover and refrigerate until serving.

Grilled Figs with Prosciutto and Goat Cheese

Years ago, a good friend of mine found this recipe, which called for small Italian plums. I tried it with local figs, and it has become one of my favorite snacks.

3/4 cup fresh chèvre, crumbled
2 tablespoons freshly grated Parmesan cheese
1/2 teaspoon herbes de Provence
8 ripe Mission figs, or any fresh figs
8 thin slices prosciutto
Extra virgin olive oil
Freshly cracked black pepper

Prepare a fire in a charcoal grill or preheat a gas grill.

In a bowl, mix the chèvre, Parmesan, and herbes de Provence thoroughly and divide into 16 small balls. Halve the figs and press the cheese balls into their centers. Halve the prosciutto slices and wrap each fig tightly. Brush with oil and dust with pepper. Grill quickly over high heat until grill marks appear, 30 to 45 seconds per side.

WD's Spicy Smoky Corn Bread

Chef Walter Dasher of 45 South gave me this recipe, and it is the best corn bread I've ever had. It may seem like too much work, but it's definitely worth it!

4 ears fresh corn
1 tablespoon canola oil
10 strips smoked bacon
$^1/_2$ large Vidalia onion, chopped
$^3/_4$ cup all-purpose flour
1$^1/_4$ cups cornmeal
2$^1/_2$ teaspoons baking powder
2 tablespoons firmly packed light brown sugar
$^1/_2$ teaspoon salt
1 cup milk
1 egg
2 or 3 chipotle chiles, chopped

Preheat the oven to 425°. Lightly oil the ears of corn with the canola oil and roast in the oven for 8 to 10 minutes, until light golden brown, then scrape the kernels from the cobs. Grease a cast-iron skillet with canola oil and put it into the hot oven. In another skillet, cook the bacon over medium heat for 8 to 10 minutes, until crisp. Reserving 1 tablespoon of the bacon fat in the skillet, transfer the remainder to a bowl. Remove and chop the bacon strips, and reserve. Sauté the onion over medium-high heat in the 1 tablespoon of fat for 4 to 6 minutes, until translucent. Reserve.

Sift together the flour, cornmeal, baking powder, sugar, and salt. In a separate bowl, combine the milk, egg, and reserved bacon fat. Stir in the corn, bacon, onion, and chiles. Combine the wet and dry ingredients, stirring by hand until just combined—do not overmix. Transfer the batter to the preheated skillet and bake for 20 to 25 minutes, until golden brown.

Native Americans shared with colonists the first recipes for corn bread, also known as hoecake, ash-cake, dodgers, and pone. It is likely that the earliest forms of corn bread were made with cornmeal, water, salt, and wild animal grease, such as bear. As living standards improved, flour, eggs, milk, baking soda, and sometimes pork cracklings were added to the recipe. There is evidence that corn bread sustained some families in the hungry years during and after the Civil War.

Strawberry Mint Sweet Tea

Once you learn how to make sweet tea, the "wine of the South," the options are endless. This is one of my favorites. Roasting the strawberries intensifies their flavor. Experiment with different types of tea; Chinese black tea and green tea are good choices.

2 pints fresh strawberries, stemmed but not hulled
1 gallon water
1 cup sugar
1½ ounces loose tea
A good handful of fresh mint
Zest of 1 lemon
1 (1 by 3-inch) piece fresh ginger, peeled and chopped

Preheat the oven to 350°. Put the strawberries in a roasting pan and roast for 12 minutes, until very dark red—almost brown—and very soft. Boil the water in a large pot and stir in the sugar to dissolve. Combine the strawberries, tea, mint, lemon zest, and ginger in a large glass pitcher, add the sugared water, and let steep. Remove the tea when the desired strength is achieved, but the fruit can be left in as long as you like—the flavor only improves and does not become bitter. Pour through a fine-meshed sieve, and serve immediately over ice or refrigerate.

Walter Dasher's Coconut Fudge Brownies

Walter Dasher's grandparents' maid baked these for Walter's fishing trips with his grandfather on the Ogeechee River when he was a boy. Walter brought me a batch for our first fishing trip on the Ford Plantation, and I was impressed by their rich flavor and ease of preparation. For chewy brownies, undercook slightly.

3/4 cup unsalted butter

10 ounces bittersweet chocolate

5 large eggs

1 3/4 cups sugar

2 1/2 cups all-purpose flour

1/2 teaspoon baking powder

1/2 teaspoon salt

1 cup shredded coconut

Preheat the oven to 350°. Grease a large round baking pan with butter. Over high heat, bring water to a boil in the bottom of a double boiler. Decrease the heat to low and melt the butter and chocolate in the top of the double boiler, stirring constantly. Set aside to cool. With an electric mixer on medium speed, whip the eggs and sugar until fluffy and light in texture and color, then combine with the cooled chocolate mixture. Sift in the flour, baking powder, and salt and mix well. Fold in the coconut and transfer the batter to the prepared pan. Bake for 25 to 35 minutes, until a toothpick comes out clean. Allow to cool before cutting.

Chef Bernard McDonough's
Plantation Game Dinner

Serves 8

❦

*"This elegant meal is designed for the most accomplished of cooks.
Try one or two recipes alone before attempting the entire meal.
It's a day-long process, even for me."*

❦

Grilled Peach Teriyaki Squab

Chorizo, Lentil, and Potato Ragout

Potato-Crusted Striped Bass with Spinach, Onions,
Bacon, and Wild Blueberry–Horseradish Vinaigrette

Roasted Rack of Venison with Wild Mushrooms and Acorn Squash–Wild Rice Risotto

Chocolate Banana Pecan Upside-Down Cake with
Coconut Ice Cream and Persimmon Syrup

❦

I then came to a small plantation by the side of another swamp: the people were remarkably civil and hospitable. The man's name was M'Intosh, a family of the first colony established in Georgia, under the conduct of General Oglethorpe. Was there ever such a scene of primitive simplicity, as was here exhibited, since the days of good king Tammany! The venerable grey-headed Caledonian smilingly meets me coming up to his house. 'Welcome, stranger; come in, and rest; the air is now very sultry; it is a very hot day.'

—WILLIAM BARTRAM (1773)

Away from Savannah's thriving port, historic homes, and beautiful squares are the remnants of Savannah's plantations, where owners created a culture of self-sufficiency for their families and the servants who tended their cotton fields or rice beds.

Those who lived on plantations made the most of their wooded surroundings. They found the forest full of peaches, figs, and game—bison, bear, deer, and birds. The shooting party became a way to entertain visitors, and the resulting game provisioned the dinner table, as did the harvests of the fields, gardens, and orchards. If the plantation happened to be located on one of the many saltwater creeks that dot the area, blue crab, oysters, shrimp, and fish were added to the menu.

It was on these plantations that some of the South's most distinctive cooking developed—back-of-the-stove dishes that were left to simmer all day with a strip of salt pork while people went about their chores. When times were tough, as in the years following the Civil War, Southerners consumed what game they could shoot and what vegetables they could grow—sweet potatoes, collard and turnip greens, okra, squash, black-eyed peas, tomatoes, eggplant, and corn. This period represented the real indoctrination of the Southern palate with vegetables: prior to the war, wealthier Americans had considered many vegetables to be the food of the poor.

But when times were good, the plantation table was filled to overflowing with good things from the fields, forests, and rivers. Chef Bernard McDonough of the Ford Plantation has created a menu reminding us of those good times.

Grilled Peach Teriyaki Squab

This dish is composed of complementary flavors: the soy sauce brings out the flavor of the fruit, and the spice brings out the sweetness of the honey. (Squab is a dark meat; cooked properly, it will still appear bright red.)

1 cup soy sauce
¼ cup hoisin sauce
1 large ripe peach, peeled and chopped
1 tablespoon chile paste
¼ cup honey
¼ cup light sesame oil
4 squab, deboned, halved, and wings removed

Combine the soy sauce, hoisin sauce, peach, chile paste, honey, and oil in a saucepan and bring to a boil over medium heat, stirring constantly. Decrease the heat to low and simmer for 5 minutes. Purée in a blender, strain through a fine-meshed sieve, and allow to cool. Marinate the squab in the mixture and refrigerate for 30 to 45 minutes.

Prepare a fire in a charcoal grill or preheat a gas grill.

Grill the squab, skin side down, over medium-high heat for 3 to 4 minutes, turn, and cook for 1 minute on the other side for medium-rare. Serve over the Chorizo, Lentil, and Potato Ragout (recipe follows).

Chorizo, Lentil, and Potato Ragout

This hearty side dish appeals to the Southern affection for sausage, beans, and potatoes and is a perfect accompaniment to any game.

Brown Veal Stock
Makes 1 gallon
8 pounds veal bones
1 pound celery, coarsely chopped
1 pound carrots, coarsely chopped
1 pound onions, peeled and coarsely chopped
6 quarts water

4 Yukon Gold potatoes, diced in 1/2-inch pieces
2 tablespoons canola or olive oil
1 cup dried black lentils
2 cups water
1 cup dried chorizo, diced into 1/2-inch pieces
1 large Vidalia onion, diced
Salt
Freshly ground black pepper

To make the stock, preheat the oven to 250°. Put the bones in a large roasting pan and roast for 5 hours. Add the celery, carrots, and onions and continue to roast for 1 more hour. Transfer the bones and vegetables to a stockpot and cover with the water. Simmer over medium heat for 4 to 6 hours, skimming off any foam that appears on the surface. Strain through a fine-meshed sieve and allow to cool. (Leftover stock can be frozen in ice-cube trays and used later for flavoring in sauces, gravies, and soups. Beef bones may be substituted to make beef stock.)

Preheat the oven to 350°. In a small bowl, mix the potatoes in the oil until they are coated. In a small roasting pan or ovenproof skillet, roast the potatoes until fork tender, about 30 minutes.

Rinse the lentils thoroughly. Bring the water, lightly salted, to a boil over medium-high heat, add the lentils, and stir. Decrease the heat to low and simmer, stirring frequently, until tender, about 20 minutes.

In a saucepan over medium-high heat, boil 3 cups of the stock for 8 to 10 minutes, until reduced to about 1 cup. Remove from the heat and set aside.

"The land belongs to the women, and the corn that grows upon it; but meat must be got by the men, because it is they only that hunt. This makes marriage necessary, that the women may furnish corn and the men meat. They also have fruit-trees in their gardens, viz. Peaches, nectarines and locusts, melons and watermelons; potatoes, pumpkins, and onions, &c. in plenty, and many kinds of fruits; as parsimonies, grapes, chinquepins, and hickory-nuts, of which they make oil."
— James Oglethorpe on Savannah's Native Americans (1733)

In a skillet, sauté the chorizo and onion over medium-high heat until the onion starts to brown slightly, about 4 minutes. Add the potatoes and lentils and sauté, stirring occasionally, for about 20 minutes, until fork tender. Add the reduced stock, stir, and remove from the heat, keeping warm. Season with salt and pepper to taste. Serve with the Grilled Peach Teriyaki Squab.

Potato-Crusted Striped Bass with Spinach, Onions, Bacon, and Wild Blueberry–Horseradish Vinaigrette

This dish was created for the guests at the Ford Plantation who enjoy fishing for bass in the well-stocked lake (too bad the Plantation has a catch-and-release policy!). This is a delicious way of preparing the ones that didn't get away.

Braised Slab Bacon
2 cups Brown Veal Stock *(page 50)*
10 ounces slab bacon

Caramelized Onions
2 tablespoons unsalted butter
3 Vidalia onions, julienned

Wild Blueberry–Horseradish Vinaigrette
$^1/_4$ cup wild blueberries if available (domestic blueberries may be substituted)
$^1/_4$ cup blackberry or peach vinegar
1 tablespoon whole-grain mustard
1 tablespoon prepared horseradish
1 tablespoon honey
1 shallot, chopped
$^1/_2$ teaspoon dried marjoram
$^1/_2$ teaspoon dried thyme
1 tablespoon pumpkin seed oil
$^1/_2$ cup canola oil
Salt
Freshly ground black pepper

Potato-Crusted Striped Bass

I egg
1/4 cup milk
8 (4-ounce) fillets striped bass
Salt
Freshly ground black pepper
I cup all-purpose flour
2 potatoes, grated
1/2 cup clarified butter *(page 112)* or vegetable oil

8 cups baby spinach

Preheat the oven to 300°. To prepare the bacon, boil the stock in a saucepan over medium-high heat for 6 to 8 minutes, until reduced to about 1 cup. In a small roasting pan, roast the bacon for 20 minutes. The bacon will shrink and become brown on the outside. Add the stock and cover with aluminum foil. Decrease the oven temperature to 225° and cook for 2 hours, turning every 1/2 hour, until the bacon is soft and plump. Remove from the oven and allow to cool. Separate the meat from the fat and discard the fat. Shred and reserve the meat.

To prepare the onions, melt the butter over medium-high heat in a large sauté pan. Add the onions and cook, stirring constantly, until they start to brown, about 12 minutes. Decrease the heat to low and cook, stirring occasionally, for 20 to 25 minutes, until the onions have caramelized. Allow to cool, and reserve.

To prepare the vinaigrette, combine the blueberries, vinegar, mustard, horseradish, honey, shallot, marjoram, and thyme in a blender and purée until smooth. With the motor running, slowly drizzle in the oils and season with salt and pepper. Taste and adjust seasonings, and reserve.

To prepare the bass, preheat the oven to 350°. Thoroughly mix the egg and milk in a shallow bowl. Season the fish with salt and pepper and lightly dredge the top side of each fillet in the flour. Dip the floured side of the fish in the egg-milk mixture. Press the fish into the grated potatoes, "crusting" the top side. Heat the clarified butter in an ovenproof skillet over medium heat. Add the fish, potato side down, and sauté for 2 1/2 minutes, until golden brown. Flip the fish over and place the pan in the oven until fish is opaque and no longer firm, 4 to 6 minutes depending on the fillets' thickness. Fish should flake when pressed (gently, so as not to ruin the presentation).

To serve, combine the spinach, caramelized onions, and bacon in a bowl and slowly drizzle in the vinaigrette while tossing. Divide the salad among 8 plates and top each with a piece of fish.

Roasted Rack of Venison with Wild Mushrooms and Açorn Squash–Wild Rice Risotto

Venison is a classic fall dish; this one has the added interest of risotto as a flavorful accompaniment.

Vegetable Stock
Makes about 5 quarts
1/4 cup vegetable oil
1 small onion, coarsely chopped
2 small carrots, coarsely chopped
1 large leek, bottom only, coarsely chopped
1/4 head cabbage, coarsely chopped
1 small turnip, coarsely chopped
1 tomato, coarsely chopped
3 cloves garlic, peeled and crushed
5 quarts water
Fresh herbs of choice (rosemary, sage, thyme, tarragon)

Venison
3 Frenched venison racks (about 9 pounds), silver skin removed
Salt
Freshly ground black pepper
Canola oil, for searing

Acorn Squash–Wild Rice Risotto
8 tablespoons unsalted butter
6 shallots, minced
2 cups arborio rice
6 cups beef stock (see *Brown Veal Stock, page 50*)
1 cup wild rice
3 softball-size acorn squashes, peeled and diced into 1/2-inch pieces
2 tablespoons fresh rosemary, chopped
2 tablespoons fresh thyme, chopped
Salt
Freshly ground black pepper

Mushrooms

2 tablespoons unsalted butter
2 pounds assorted wild mushrooms, cleaned but not rinsed, coarsely chopped

To prepare the vegetable stock, heat the oil in a large pot over medium heat. Add the onion, carrots, leek, cabbage, turnip, tomato, and garlic and sweat for 5 minutes. Cover with the water, add the herbs, and simmer over medium heat for 1 hour. Strain through a fine-meshed sieve and allow to cool. (This stock freezes well for later use. Other vegetable scraps can be used as well, for example, mushroom stems.)

To prepare the venison, preheat the oven to 325°. Season the racks liberally with salt and pepper. Lightly oil a large sauté pan with canola oil. Add the venison and sear over high heat, 1 minute per side, until slightly crisp and brown. Transfer to a roasting pan and roast the racks in the oven, ribs down, for 20 minutes, until a meat thermometer inserted into the eye of the roast registers an internal temperature of 125°. Remove from the oven, cover with foil, and keep warm.

(continued)

To prepare the risotto, melt 2 tablespoons of the butter in a heavy saucepan over medium heat. Add the shallots and sauté for 3 minutes, until golden. Add the arborio rice and stir until coated with butter. Add 1 cup of the beef stock and stir until absorbed. Add another cup every 4 or 5 minutes, stirring until all is absorbed, 20 to 25 minutes. Remove from heat and reserve.

In a saucepan over medium-high heat, bring 2 cups of the vegetable stock to a boil, add the wild rice, decrease the heat to low, cover, and simmer until just tender, about 30 minutes. In a skillet, melt 2 tablespoons of the butter over medium heat. Add the squash and sauté for 3 to 4 minutes, until tender and starting to brown. Add the wild rice, squash, rosemary, and thyme to the risotto. Stir in the remaining 4 tablespoons butter and season to taste with salt and pepper.

To prepare the mushrooms, melt 1 tablespoon of the butter in a skillet over medium heat. Add the mushrooms in single layers and sauté for 4 minutes, until tender, adding the rest of the butter as needed, trying to stir only once (too much movement releases liquid, causing the mushrooms to become soggy).

To cut the venison into chops, hold the racks so that the ribs are standing straight up. Using the bones as a guide, cut between the ribs to create separate chops.

Place a scoop of risotto on each of 8 heated dinner plates. Top it with 2 venison chops and a serving of mushrooms.

Chocolate Banana Pecan Upside-Down Cake with Coconut Ice Cream and Persimmon Syrup

A most Southern of indulgent desserts, this one incorporates ever-popular chocolate with local pecans, tropical fruits, and an unusual syrup. Once inverted, the cake can be passed around the table with a cake server, followed by the sauce in a sauceboat and the ice cream in a prechilled serving bowl.

Chocolate Banana Pecan Upside-Down Cake

5 ounces bittersweet chocolate

³/₄ cup unsalted butter, at room temperature

¹/₂ cup granulated sugar

4 eggs

¹/₂ cup panko (Japanese white bread crumbs)

1¹/₂ cups pecans, toasted (*page 16*) and ground

4 bananas, sliced

2 tablespoons unsalted butter, melted

2 tablespoons freshly squeezed lemon juice

¹/₂ cup firmly packed brown sugar

Coconut Ice Cream

2 tablespoons granulated sugar

2 egg yolks

1 cup freshly grated coconut

¹/₄ cup heavy cream

Persimmon Syrup

8 persimmons

1 vanilla bean

2 cups white wine

1 cup granulated sugar

Preheat the oven to 350°. Wrap the bottom of a 9-inch springform pan with aluminum foil. Butter the bottom and sides of the pan.

To prepare the cake, melt the chocolate in the top of a double boiler over high heat, stirring constantly. With an electric mixer on low speed, thoroughly mix the 3/4 cup butter and granulated sugar in a bowl until pale yellow. While continuing to mix, slowly add the melted chocolate to the butter-sugar mixture. Add the eggs one at a time while mixing on medium speed. Turn off the mixer and fold in the panko and pecans. In a bowl, combine the banana slices, 2 tablespoons melted butter, lemon juice, and brown sugar and mix well. Arrange the banana slices in concentric circles in a single layer on the bottom of the prepared pan. Pour the batter over the bananas and bake for 25 to 30 minutes, or until a toothpick comes out clean. Cool on a rack, and invert onto a cake plate to unmold.

To prepare the ice cream, whisk together the sugar and egg yolks in a bowl until incorporated. In a saucepan over medium heat, combine the coconut and cream and bring to a boil. Pour a little of the hot cream into the egg mixture, then pour all of the egg mixture back into the cream. Transfer to a bowl and refrigerate until chilled, preferably overnight. Churn the mixture in an ice-cream maker according to the manufacturer's instructions.

To prepare the syrup, preheat the oven to 350°. Put the persimmons in a roasting pan and roast for 30 minutes, until soft and dull brownish orange. Allow to cool, then dice. With a sharp knife, cut the vanilla bean lengthwise and scrape out the seeds. In a saucepan over medium heat, combine the persimmons, vanilla seeds and pod, wine, and sugar. Bring to a boil, decrease the heat to low, and simmer uncovered for 10 to 15 minutes until the persimmon pieces fall apart. Remove and discard the vanilla pod. Pass through a food mill while hot, and purée in a blender until smooth.

Serve as described in the headnote or, for a more formal presentation, ladle a small pool of the syrup onto the center of a dessert plate. Place the point of a slice of the cake at the very edge of the pool, and place a scoop of ice cream beside the cake.

PURVEYORS

If you have difficulty acquiring some of the necessary ingredients for these menus, the following purveyors can be relied upon to help you.

D'Artagnan
800-327-8246
This is a wonderful source for mushrooms, truffles, foie gras, and wild game.

The Grateful Palate
888-472-5283
Specialty items, such as pumpkin seed oil, are available here.

Dean and Deluca
800-221-7714
This is a great source for specialty foods and equipment.

Chef George Spriggs's
Beach Party

Serves 8

❦

"I love Tybee Island because of the attitude—the combination of a gorgeous setting, local seafood, and friendly people makes it the ideal place to dine. There's no pressure here to dress to the nines or show off your etiquette. People bask in the healthy, romantic air of the island. To dine feet away from the ocean, the only lights coming from candles and the stars, is about as good as it gets. My guests sometimes dance on the beach after dinner. Not many restaurants can boast that."

❦

Oven-Roasted, Barbecued Baby Back Ribs

Herb-Infused Rock Cornish Game Hens

Caribbean-Spiced Boiled Shrimp

Southern-Style Potato Salad

Asparagus, Red Onion, and Roasted Pine Nut Salad with
Lemon and Rice Wine Vinegar

❦

Although the fish stalls in the City market are filled with crabs and shrimp brought in fresh daily, the majority of Savannah housekeepers prefer to buy their sea foods from the negro hucksters who come in from the neighboring watering places, and peddle their wares from door to door—carrying on their heads great baskets of shrimp and crabs and oysters, and filling the morning air with their familiar cry: 'Crab by'er! Yeh Swimps! Yeh Oshta!'

—HARRIET ROSS COLQUITT, *THE SAVANNAH COOKBOOK* (1933)

Eighteen miles and a mindset away from Savannah is Tybee Island, a slice of sand two and a half miles long and two-thirds of a mile wide, where for 150 years Savannahians have gone to stroll, swim, boat, and picnic.

Tybee is one of a series of barrier islands—including Wassaw, Ossabaw, St. Catherine's, Blackbeard, Sapelo, St. Simons, Jekyll, and Cumberland—that are significant to the area for several reasons. Located on the Atlantic Flyway, they offer respite to migrating waterfowl. Also, as the name implies, the islands buffer the inland from coastal storms. Most importantly, behind the islands are acres upon acres of tidal creeks and salt marshes, nurseries for many species of marine life.

Aside from its ecological importance, Tybee offers visitors a feast of sight and sound—gentle dunes, wild sea oats, palmettos, and the low roar of the Atlantic breaking on the beach. Pelicans hang lazily over the waves, sailboats loll on the horizon, and the rolling backs of dolphins sometimes surface in the sunset. Giant container ships, carrying cargo from around the world, sit patiently in the Atlantic Ocean, awaiting the proper tides to enter the Savannah River channel leading to Savannah's port. Tybee Island Lighthouse stands silent guard at the mouth of the Savannah River, a position it has held since 1736. Near the south end of the beach is a grand pier, Tybrisia Pavilion, where locals fish by day and listen to musical groups ranging from high school choirs to rock bands in the evenings.

Shoes are optional just about everywhere on Tybee, although shirts are typically required. The biggest event of the year for locals is the Beach Bum Parade, hosted by water pistol–toting locals. It might be said that Tybee is the antithesis of mannerly Savannah—barefoot, tousled, and overly friendly, the type of place where one might be invited on the spot to sample a plate of barbecued baby back ribs at George Spriggs's North Beach Grill, situated right on the beach not far from the Tybee Island Lighthouse.

Oven-Roasted, Barbecued Baby Back Ribs

Baby back ribs are more versatile than regular spareribs; they are less fatty, and they're especially suited for a picnic because they can be served hot or cold. Though they are not cooked on a grill, the ribs in this recipe end up barbecued nevertheless by being roasted in an oven.

3 full slabs baby back ribs (about 1 1/2 pounds)
1/4 cup red wine vinegar
Seasoned salt
Freshly ground black pepper
1 yellow onion, sliced in thin circles
3 canned chipotle chiles in adobo sauce, finely diced, sauce reserved
1 1/2 cups hickory-smoked barbecue sauce
Juice of 1/2 lime

Preheat the oven to 400°. Rinse the ribs and remove all excess fat from the backs of the slabs. Put the ribs in a large Dutch oven or baking dish. Pour the vinegar over the slabs, making sure every surface is moistened, then coat each layer with a thin, even layer of salt, and then of pepper. Layer the onion slices onto the ribs. Cover with aluminum foil and roast for 2 1/2 hours. The ribs should be extremely tender when done, and the onions will adhere to the meat. Test the tenderness of the meat by applying gentle pressure with a fork against the bone of the end piece; meat should fall away from the bone.

Put the chiles, all of the adobo sauce from the can, barbecue sauce, and lime juice in a bowl. Mix well. Transfer the ribs and onions to a flat baking sheet or a new baking dish and coat each slab with the barbecue sauce mixture. Put the ribs back into the oven for 30 minutes, uncovered. When they're done, the corners of the ribs will begin to darken and the sauce will be baked onto the ribs.

To serve, cut each rack into individual ribs.

Herb-Infused Rock Cornish Game Hens

Rock Cornish game hens are a fancy version of the Southern staple, chicken. They are particularly tender and hold their flavor better than fryers or roasters. This recipe uses fresh herbs from the garden. Left crusted on the bird at serving time, the herbs provide a delicate touch of freshness.

4 plump Rock Cornish game hens
Juice of 2 lemons
¼ cup fresh sage, chopped
½ cup cilantro, chopped
¼ cup fresh thyme, chopped
¼ cup fresh basil, chopped
¼ cup extra virgin olive oil
6 to 8 large cloves garlic, minced
Salt
Freshly ground black pepper
¼ cup vegetable oil

Cut the hens in half and then into quarters—two leg quarters and two breast quarters. Remove the breast bones. Rinse and dry the hen quarters and put them in a wide, shallow dish. Pour the lemon juice over, making sure to coat all the surfaces. Combine the fresh herbs in a bowl. Spread half of the olive oil, half of the garlic, and half of the fresh herb mixture evenly over the surface of a rimmed baking sheet. Place the hen portions on top. Generously coat the hens with salt, pepper, and the remaining garlic. Spread the remaining herbs over the hens and then drizzle with the remaining olive oil. Cover tightly with plastic wrap and refrigerate for 24 hours.

Preheat the oven to 400°. Heat the vegetable oil in a nonstick sauté pan over medium-high heat. Remove the hens from the baking dish and brush away any large or dangling herb pieces. Sauté for about 3 minutes per side, until brown. Place the hens and the herb, garlic, and oil marinade in a baking dish or Dutch oven, cover, and roast for 40 minutes, until the skin is golden to dark brown and crisp at the edges and the internal temperature registers 150° on a meat thermometer. The herbs should become dark but should not be burnt.

Serve two hen quarters (a leg and a breast) to each person.

Caribbean-Spiced Boiled Shrimp

Even the most conservative Savannah diner can appreciate this creative twist on a traditional regional favorite.

1 tablespoon black peppercorns
1 tablespoon red peppercorns
1 tablespoon green peppercorns
1 tablespoon whole cloves
2 (4-inch) cinnamon sticks
1 tablespoon whole cardamom seeds
2 lemons
2 limes
1 orange
2 quarts water
2 cups freshly squeezed orange juice
1 cup red wine
4 large bay leaves
3 tablespoons Paul Prudhomme's Seafood Magic
3 pounds jumbo shrimp (21 to 25 count), shells on
Lettuce, for garnish

Put the peppercorns, cloves, cinnamon sticks, and cardamom seeds in a large stockpot and begin to heat over medium heat, stirring the ingredients periodically. Slice 1 lemon, 1 lime, and the orange into rounds. Add the sliced fruit, water, orange juice, wine, bay leaves, and spice mix to the stockpot. Bring to a boil and continue to boil, uncovered, until the liquid has reduced by about 1 inch, about 20 minutes. Decrease the heat to low, add the shrimp, and cook until pink, 2 to 3 minutes. Place a colander over a large bowl and drain the shrimp as soon as they're done, reserving the solids. (You may use the liquid as a shrimp stock.) Lay the shrimp on a bed of ice on a platter lined with lettuce, or arrange shrimp on beds of lettuce on each of 8 dinner plates.

To serve, arrange the cooked fruits, peppercorns, cloves, and cinnamon over the shrimp. Slice the remaining lemon and lime, and garnish the shrimp with them.

Shrimping is a prosperous industry in Savannah's surrounding Low Country, where shrimp boats trawl the Atlantic from Florida to the Carolinas. Until refrigeration methods were widely adopted in the early 1930s, however, most shrimp were consumed only in coastal regions due to their perishability. The amount of shrimp consumed in the United States has doubled in the last decade to more than 1 billion pounds a year, making it one of most popular seafoods in the nation, second only to tuna.

Southern-Style Potato Salad

Most prefer this traditional dish cold, but it is also delicious at room temperature. The key to good potato salad is to have a light touch with the mustard.

3 pounds white potatoes, peeled and cut into large cubes
3 eggs
5 stalks celery, diced
¹/₂ cup sweet pickle relish
¹/₂ tablespoon prepared mustard
¹/₃ cup high-quality mayonnaise
Salt
Freshly ground black pepper

Put the potatoes and eggs in a large pot and pour in water to cover. Bring to a boil over medium-high heat and cook 15 to 20 minutes, until the potatoes are just tender. (Eggs may be removed after 10 minutes if you prefer a softer yolk, or left in with the potatoes.) Drain the potatoes and put them in a large bowl to cool. Peel and chop the eggs and combine with the potatoes. Add the celery, pickle relish, and mustard and mix well. Add the mayonnaise and mix well. Season with salt and pepper and mix again. Let cool to room temperature, then cover and refrigerate for 2 hours before serving (or you may serve the salad at room temperature).

There were many reasons to favor hogs over other forms of livestock. First, hogs were inexpensive to maintain and relatively self-sufficient, foraging on scraps, street garbage, and woodland fodder. Second, pigs can increase their weight 150 times in the first year of life, unlike the much slower-growing cow. Third, almost all of the animal could be used for food and rendered in many forms, including hams, sausages, cracklings, and cooking lard. Preserved pork in the form of salt pork sustained a population of Southerners during the hard times of the Civil War and, later, the Depression. Though beef and chicken have replaced pork in popularity across the nation, barbecued pork remains one of the favorite dishes of the South.

Asparagus, Red Onion, and Roasted Pine Nut Salad with Lemon and Rice Wine Vinegar

This is a great way to wake up the tastebuds, so it can be an effective first course. The red onions add heat to the cool asparagus.

¹/₄ cup pine nuts
2 tablespoons olive oil
1 bunch thick fresh asparagus (about 20 stalks), trimmed
¹/₂ red onion, julienned
Juice of 1 lemon
1 tablespoon rice wine vinegar
Salt
Freshly ground black pepper

Preheat the oven to 325°. Put the pine nuts in a small roasting pan with the olive oil, and roast, turning at 1 minute, until golden brown, a total of about 2 minutes.

Bring a pot of water to a boil over medium-high heat. Turn off the heat and add the asparagus. Blanch for 1 minute, until bright green. Drain, then immerse in ice or cold water to halt the cooking, and drain again. In a bowl, mix the asparagus, onion, and lemon juice together.

Drizzle the vinegar over the asparagus-onion mixture, season with salt and pepper, and toss to coat evenly. Add the pine nuts and toss again.

To serve, ladle the salad onto a serving platter with a fork and spoon.

Chef George Spriggs's

Formal Symphony Dinner

Serves 4

❧❦❧

"I am a classical music fan, and I find this menu an elegant beginning to an evening of fine food and great music."

❧❦❧

Golden Pineapple with Lime, Lime Zest, and Rum

Sherry-Laced Mushroom Soup

Marinated, Roasted Squid Stuffed with Spinach, Shallots, and Roasted Pine Nuts

Pan-Seared Halibut with Jasmine Rice, Shrimp, and Tomato Concassée

Boston Lettuce, Radicchio, Water Chestnuts, Bamboo Shoots, and Sugar Snap Peas with Orange Juice–Port Wine Dressing

Banana Custard with Semisweet Chocolate

❧❦❧

Soup should be a daily dish at the board; it can be made in small or large quantities, and if prepared with care is acceptable and nutritious, particularly to the aged, who have no longer the full powers of mastication.

—MRS. GOODFELLOW'S COOKERY AS IT SHOULD BE: A NEW MANUAL OF THE DINING ROOM AND KITCHEN (1865)

For many years, the dinner party was *the* way Savannah entertained. It was a time to show off the heirloom silver, china, and crystal on grandmother's antique dining table, an opportunity to serve up the finest food one could order in or create, and a chance to bring together a cast of colorful characters with whom to socialize, strategize, or categorize. "You go to a Savannah dinner party, and you may as well be at the theater," explains Savannah native and writer Arthur Gordon, a favorite dinner party guest, along with his wife, Pam.

Savannah has always loved to throw a dinner party for special guests. When President McKinley visited in December of 1898, he was served oysters on the half shell, green turtle soup, salmon, beef tenderloin, sweetbreads, Georgia terrapin, roasted Chatham County partridge, asparagus, potatoes, Chatham Artillery punch, coffee, and crème de menthe, followed, of course, by cigars and cigarettes.

What remains important even today is not just the menu—which still must offer up what is freshest, best, and most local—but the fact that Savannahians still want to present the finest they have in the most beautiful setting possible, served with great hospitality.

Golden Pineapple with Lime, Lime Zest, and Rum

This entremet bears a Caribbean and African-American influence, combining fruit and spice. The refreshing pineapple and lime cleanse the palate, and the rum adds a contrasting piquancy, delivering an intensely pleasurable experience. If a regular pineapple is used, four times as much sugar will be required.

1 golden pineapple, peeled, cored, and diced
Zest from 1 1/2 limes
Juice of 1 lime
1 tablespoon sugar
3 tablespoons high-quality white rum

Put the pineapple in a bowl with the lime zest and lime juice, and mix well. Add the sugar and rum and mix again. Cover and refrigerate for 4 hours before serving.

Sherry-Laced Mushroom Soup

This dish, based on one of the most earthy ingredients, mushrooms, makes a perfect first course in Savannah. The simple mushroom lends itself to manipulation, but the challenge is to not destroy its delicate flavor. This is why care is taken to simmer, not boil, the soup once the mushrooms are added.

Chicken Stock
Makes 2 quarts

2 chicken backs
5 quarts water
4 chicken necks
4 chicken gizzards
7 large onions, diced
7 celery stalks, diced
Salt
Freshly ground black pepper

Roux

$1/4$ cup unsalted butter
$1/2$ cup all-purpose flour

$1/4$ cup sherry
$1/3$ cup heavy cream
1 pound mixed mushrooms, chopped
$1/4$ pound whole oyster mushrooms
$1/4$ pound whole shiitake mushrooms
$1/4$ pound whole enoki mushrooms

To prepare the stock, heat a large stockpot over high heat. Add the chicken backs, decrease the heat to medium-high, and sear for 3 minutes on each side until golden brown. Add the water, necks, gizzards, onions, and celery, season with salt and pepper, and cook, covered, over medium heat for 2 hours. Strain the stock through a fine-meshed sieve and discard the solids.

To prepare the roux, melt the butter in a skillet over high heat. With a whisk, stir in the flour gradually until the mixture becomes pastelike, about 2 minutes. Continue cooking over low heat, stirring constantly, until the roux turns a caramel color, about 5 minutes. Do not allow to burn or scorch. (Roux must be watched and stirred until done; do not leave it unattended.)

In a stockpot, bring the stock to a low boil over medium-high heat. Decrease the heat to medium. Add the sherry and cream, decrease the heat to medium-low, and simmer for about 5 minutes. Whisk in the roux. Add the chopped mushrooms and continue to simmer for about 10 minutes; the mushrooms should retain their shape, and the soup should thicken enough so that the back of a spoon dipped into it comes out completely coated. Reserve 4 of each of the three kinds of whole mushrooms. Add the remaining whole mushrooms to the stock and simmer for another 10 minutes. Ladle into individual serving bowls and place three whole mushrooms—one of each kind—in the center. Serve hot.

Marinated, Roasted Squid Stuffed with Spinach, Shallots, and Roasted Pine Nuts

Most diners are more familiar with fried squid than they are with roasted. Squid tubes (also known as hoods) are the fleshy outsides of the squids' bodies. In this recipe, they are stuffed and served whole, with crostini or toasted, sliced French bread. The delicious marinade is what sets this dish apart.

Juice of 1 lemon
1 teaspoon salt
3 serrano chiles, quartered
1/2 bunch cilantro, chopped
2 teaspoons lemongrass, chopped
4 or 5 large cloves garlic, chopped
12 squid tubes, cleaned
1 tablespoon olive oil
1 shallot, diced
3 cups fresh spinach leaves
Salt
Freshly ground black pepper
1/2 cup whole pine nuts, roasted (*page 69*)
Julienned spinach, for garnish

Prepare the marinade by combining the lemon juice, salt, chiles, cilantro, half of the lemongrass, and half of the garlic in a shallow, nonreactive dish. Lightly score each squid tube two to three times horizontally, place in the marinade, turn to coat, cover, and refrigerate overnight.

To prepare the stuffing, heat the olive oil in a skillet over medium heat. Add the shallot and the remaining garlic and sauté for 2 minutes, until the shallot becomes translucent. Add the spinach and the remaining lemongrass. Allow the spinach to wilt for about 1 minute, then season with salt and pepper, add 1/4 cup of the pine nuts, and remove from the heat.

Prepare a fire in a charcoal grill or preheat a gas grill, and preheat the oven to 350°. Grease a small baking dish with oil. Remove the squid tubes from the marinade. Stuff each tube three-quarters full with the spinach and pine nut mixture. Close the ends of the tubes with wooden skewers. Place the stuffed squid on the grill for 30 seconds per side, just long enough to obtain grill marks. Transfer the squid to the prepared baking dish and place in the oven for 5 minutes. Serve 3 per person on a bed of julienned spinach. Garnish with the remaining 1/4 cup pine nuts.

Pan-Seared Halibut with Jasmine Rice, Shrimp, and Tomato Concassée

Halibut is a pure white fish that flakes apart when cooked and makes a palatable partner with the rice served at most Low Country meals. Jasmine rice is a flavorful white rice. Both lemongrass and mint grow easily in Savannah herb gardens and make a flavorful addition to the concassée.

2 cups jasmine rice

3 1/2 cups water

6 large ripe plum tomatoes

4 (7-ounce) halibut fillets, skin on

Juice of 1 lemon

Salt

Freshly ground black pepper

6 tablespoons extra virgin olive oil

4 shallots, chopped

16 jumbo shrimp (21 to 25 count), peeled and deveined, tails on

2 or 3 large cloves garlic, minced

1 tablespoon lemongrass, chopped

Bring the rice and water to a vigorous boil over high heat, cover, and remove from the heat. Let stand, undisturbed, until completely cooked, about 20 minutes.

Preheat the oven to 350°. To make the concassée, cut each tomato in half lengthwise. With a teaspoon, scrape out the seeds in both halves of the tomato, then dice the tomatoes into small, even pieces.

To prepare the fish, dip both sides of each fillet into the lemon juice, then season with salt and pepper. Heat 4 tablespoons of the olive oil in an ovenproof skillet over medium heat. Add the shallots and sauté until translucent, about 2 minutes. Add the fillets and sear for 2 minutes on each side, until the flesh begins to brown. Put the skillet into the oven for about 15 minutes, until a fork pierces the halibut's skin and flesh cleanly.

Heat the remaining 2 tablespoons olive oil in a skillet over medium heat. Add the shrimp and garlic and sauté for 2 minutes, until the shrimp turn pink. Add the concassée, lemongrass, and mint sprig. Toss until the shrimp are pink all over. Season with salt and pepper.

To serve, place a mound of rice in the center of each plate. Place a halibut fillet atop the rice. Place 4 shrimp around the fish and rice, remove the mint sprig from the concassée, and fill in the gap between the fish and the rice with the concassée.

Boston Lettuce, Radicchio, Water Chestnuts, Bamboo Shoots, and Sugar Snap Peas with Orange Juice–Port Wine Dressing

Texture is most important in a green salad; it should be clean and refreshing. The blending of the greens with the red and white of the radicchio is pleasing to the eye. Tender Boston lettuce contrasts with the crispness of the radicchio, water chestnuts, bamboo shoots, and sugar snap peas. The port wine and orange juice provide both tart and sweet sensations.

Dressing
2 cups freshly squeezed orange juice
1 teaspoon Dijon mustard
4 tablespoons port wine
1/4 cup rice wine vinegar
1 1/2 cups extra virgin olive oil
1 shallot, diced
Salt

Salad
1/2 tablespoon olive oil
1/2 pound sugar snap peas, stemmed
1 shallot, diced
2 heads Boston lettuce
1 head radicchio
1/4 pound water chestnuts, julienned
1/4 pound bamboo shoots, julienned
1 teaspoon freshly squeezed lemon juice

To prepare the dressing, blend the orange juice, mustard, wine, and vinegar in a blender on medium speed. With the motor still running on medium speed, slowly add the olive oil. Turn off the blender and stir in the shallot. Let the dressing stand for 30 minutes at room temperature before using. Season with salt to taste.

To prepare the salad, heat the oil in a skillet over high heat. Add the peas and shallot and sauté long enough for the peas to become coated with the oil,

about 1^1/$_2$ minutes. Remove from the heat. Arrange the lettuce and radicchio on 4 salad plates. Top with the peas, water chestnuts, and bamboo shoots. Drizzle with the lemon juice and then ladle the dressing over each serving; do not toss.

Banana Custard with Semisweet Chocolate

This recipe is a fond variation on one of my mother's desserts—a childhood favorite. The combination of flavor and texture brings together country comfort and city sophistication.

1 cup sugar
$^1/_2$ cup all-purpose flour
6 eggs, separated
$2^1/_4$ cups evaporated milk
1 teaspoon vanilla extract
4 (1-ounce) pieces semisweet chocolate
1 (12-ounce) box vanilla wafers
5 to 7 ripe bananas, sliced
Chocolate chips, for garnish

In the top of a double boiler over boiling water, mix $^2/_3$ cup of the sugar, the flour, and the egg yolks. As the mixture begins to warm, stir in the milk. Stir constantly until the custard begins to thicken, about 10 minutes. Stir in the vanilla extract and remove from the heat.

In a second double boiler, melt the chocolate, stirring constantly. Spoon 3 tablespoons of the custard into the bottom of a round 4-quart casserole dish. Top with one-third of the wafers and then one-third of the banana slices. Spoon on about one-third of the remaining custard, and drizzle on one-third of the melted chocolate. Repeat this process until you have three layers each of wafers and bananas, and end with a layer of custard and chocolate. Whether you use the entire box of wafers will depend on how tightly you pack the layers.

Preheat the oven to 350°. Combine the egg whites and the remaining $^1/_3$ cup sugar in a bowl and whip with an electric mixer on medium speed until the egg whites are stiff enough to hold onto the sides of the bowl without slipping when the bowl is tilted. Spoon the egg whites onto the custard. Bake for 10 minutes, until the egg whites begin to brown. Refrigerate for 1 hour.

To serve, scoop out with a large serving spoon. Sprinkle with chocolate chips for garnish.

Chef Susan Mason's

Wormsloe Plantation Picnic

Serves 10 to 12

❧

"What better way to enjoy local seafood and vegetables than a summertime picnic at romantic Wormsloe Plantation?"

❧

Potato and Corn Salad with Buttermilk Dressing

Crab Cakes with Tarragon Tartar Sauce

Pickled Shrimp

Tomato Sandwiches

Grilled Vegetable Marinade

Blackberry Cake with Seven-Minute Frosting

Sangria

❧

March 20, 1880—Leta had a luncheon party at Wormsloe. They went by rail relieved by carriages. (Gave the Steward of the Wyoming $5.00 for a case of butter.) At the luncheon, Josiah Murray and brother waited. Annie Nuthall, Mathilda and Katherine in the kitchen. Oyster on the shell, boned turkey truffled, sandwiches, crab salad, and orange sherbet, cakes, strawberries, oranges, apples, prunes, dried ginger, coffee, burnt almonds, chocolate caramels. Wine, even sherry and champagne. Weather charming.

—GEORGE WYMBERLEY JONES
DE RENNE JOURNAL (1880)

Just ten miles from downtown Savannah, at the end of a mile-long alley of magnificent live oaks, are the tabby ruins of Wormsloe, the colonial estate of Nobel Jones. (Tabby is a cement made of sand, gravel, or limestone and oyster shells; it was used extensively throughout the Low Country in the seventeenth and eighteenth centuries.) Jones arrived in Savannah with James Oglethorpe aboard the ship *Anne* in 1733, and he was one of only a handful of the original settlers to survive in the new Georgia colony. Nearby is a plantation house, built in 1828, that continues to be the private home of Jones's descendants. Wormsloe's ruins and nature trails are operated by the state and are open to the public.

Visitors to Wormsloe are often seen at the gates to the property, cameras poised to capture the romantic symmetry of the live oak drive. Early spring is an especially beautiful time for a stroll or picnic, particularly if the Civil War–era camellias, wisteria, magnolia, or dogwood are in bloom. The woodsy paths wind along the Jones Narrows, which was the principal waterway from Savannah to Frederica in the eighteenth century. After 1740, Jones was entrusted with guarding the narrows against Spanish attack.

This menu provides a timeless repast at Wormsloe Plantation with a choice of traditional Low Country favorites—crab cakes, tomato sandwiches, potato and corn salad, and blackberry cake—as the basis for the picnic.

Potato and Corn Salad with Buttermilk Dressing

This is one of our favorite salads to make in summer when corn is at its very best. It is especially good if chilled overnight.

Buttermilk Dressing
1/2 cup buttermilk
2 tablespoons mayonnaise
1 tablespoon white wine vinegar

12 new potatoes
6 ears fresh yellow corn
4 tablespoons salad oil
4 tablespoons unsalted butter
4 whole scallions, chopped

To prepare the dressing, whisk all the ingredients together in a small bowl. Cover and refrigerate until chilled through, about 30 minutes.

Put the potatoes into a large pot, cover with water, and boil for 20 to 30 minutes, until fork tender. Allow to cool slightly, then peel and slice.

Scrape the kernels from the corn cobs. In a skillet, heat the oil and butter over medium heat. Add the corn kernels and sauté for 6 to 8 minutes, until bright yellow. Combine the potatoes, corn, and scallions in a large bowl. Allow to cool, then toss gently with the dressing. Cover and refrigerate for at least 2 hours before serving cold.

Crab Cakes with Tarragon Tartar Sauce

One secret to good crab cakes is to make sure that the lump crabmeat is fresh, of excellent quality, and picked clean of shells.

Tarragon Tartar Sauce

$3/4$ cup mayonnaise
$1^1/_2$ teaspoons sweet pickle relish
2 tablespoons fresh tarragon, minced

Crab Cakes

$1/2$ cup mayonnaise
2 tablespoons Dijon mustard
$2^1/_2$ teaspoons Old Bay Seasoning
$1/8$ teaspoon cayenne pepper
1 red bell pepper, seeded, deribbed, and very finely chopped
3 large egg yolks
2 pounds lump crabmeat
Dash of Worcestershire sauce
2 whole scallions, very finely chopped
5 cups cornflakes, crushed into crumbs
2 tablespoons unsalted butter
Lemon wedges, for garnish

To prepare the tartar sauce, combine the mayonnaise, relish, and tarragon in a small bowl. Cover and refrigerate until ready to serve.

To prepare the crab cakes, mix together the mayonnaise, mustard, spice mix, cayenne, bell pepper, egg yolks, crab, Worcestershire, and scallions in a large bowl. Form the mixture into 12 small patties and chill, covered, for at least 1 hour and up to 4 hours.

Preheat the oven to 350°. Gently roll the patties in the cornflakes. Transfer the cakes to a baking sheet and top each with $1/2$ teaspoon of butter. Bake for 10 minutes, until crisp. Serve steaming hot with the tartar sauce and lemon wedges.

Pickled Shrimp

At every party that I serve these, someone asks for the recipe. They are wonderful for cocktail parties as well as for picnics.

1/2 cup celery tops
1/4 cup pickling spice
4 pounds jumbo shrimp (21 to 25 count), peeled, deveined, and tails removed
3 1/2 teaspoons salt

Pickling Mixture
3 stalks celery, chopped
2 large white onions, sliced
1 1/4 cups vegetable oil
3/4 cup apple cider vinegar
2 1/2 teaspoons salt
8 bay leaves
2 1/2 tablespoons capers packed in vinegar
6 drops Tabasco sauce
1/2 green bell pepper, seeded, deribbed, and diced

To cook the shrimp, tie the celery tops and pickling spice in a cheesecloth bag. Bring a large pot of water to a boil over high heat. Place the cheesecloth bag in the water, decrease the heat to medium-low, and simmer for 10 minutes. Add the shrimp and salt and simmer for 5 minutes, or until the shrimp are pink all over. Drain.

To pickle the shrimp, combine all the pickling ingredients and the shrimp in a large, nonreactive bowl. Cover and refrigerate for 12 hours. Drain, discard the pickling mixture, and serve the shrimp on a silver platter or in a decorative ceramic bowl.

Tomato Sandwiches

I have never seen someone eat only one of these. I think the most sandwiches I ever witnessed one person consume was twenty-two at one sitting. And there was a whole lot of sitting after that!

8 ripe, *good* tomatoes, in season
80 slices white sandwich bread
1 to 1¼ cups mayonnaise
1 tablespoon Lawry's Seasoned Salt

Peel the tomatoes and slice each into 5 slices. Put them on a tray between paper towels and refrigerate overnight to drain.

Cut the bread into rounds with a 3-inch biscuit cutter. Mix together the mayonnaise and seasoned salt in a small bowl until evenly combined. Spread 2 bread rounds with the mayonnaise mixture, place a tomato slice on 1 piece of bread, and close with the other. Repeat until all the bread rounds and tomato slices are used. Arrange on a serving tray lined with doilies.

Grilled Vegetable Marinade

Grilled vegetables have become a gourmet item in many Savannah restaurants. This is our version for picnics or parties.

Few foods are as thoroughly contradictory as the "love apple," a fruit that acts like a vegetable, can be eaten green or red, is tiny or tremendous, and has been suspected both to be poisonous and to cast spells of love.

Though native to Central America, tomatoes were not widely consumed by Americans until after the Civil War, as they were believed to cause cancer, among other afflictions. But they have been enjoyed in the South since at least Jefferson's time, when "tomatas" were consumed as ketchup, in soups, with okra, and, on occasion, simply raw.

Though botanically a fruit, the tomato was ruled to be a vegetable by the Supreme Court in 1893, when the majority observed that tomatoes are "usually served at dinner in, with, or after the soup, fish or meat, which constitute the principal part of the repast, and not, like fruits, generally as dessert." Other botanical fruits ruled to be culinary vegetables included squash, cucumbers, beans, peas, eggplants, peppers, and avocados.

Everyone knows that fresh tomatoes are good only between the months of late May and early August, and that the best way to eat a tomato is raw, sliced, and seasoned with salt and pepper. Whole tomatoes should never be refrigerated, as this saps their flavor, and, if green, should ripen in a paper bag.

Marinade

¼ cup freshly squeezed lemon juice
¾ cup extra virgin olive oil
2 tablespoons red wine vinegar
4 tablespoons fresh basil, minced
1 tablespoon Dijon mustard
1 bay leaf, crumbled
½ teaspoon dried thyme
½ teaspoon dried marjoram
2 cloves garlic, minced
4 tablespoons fresh parsley, chopped
Salt
Freshly ground black pepper

6 yellow squash, cut into chunks
4 zucchini, cut into chunks
2 large onions, cut into wedges
1 pound mushroom caps
1 pound cherry tomatoes, stemmed

To prepare the marinade, combine all the ingredients and whisk until well blended. Put the vegetables in a shallow, nonreactive dish, pour the marinade over, cover, and refrigerate for at least 2 hours or overnight.

Prepare a fire in a charcoal grill or preheat a gas grill. Grill the vegetables, basting frequently with the marinade, until tender and brightly colored, about 15 minutes. Discard the marinade. Serve the vegetables on a large platter.

The space under Wormsloe's oak-lined avenue has been described as spiritual in nature, evoking the air of a great cathedral. The mile-long trail winds through a canopy of light and shadow, where twisting limbs reach like gothic arches toward the sky. Cascades of Spanish moss float from the leaves like swamp tinsel. A fertile imagination is not required to envision mild ghosts slipping through the trees, denizens of ages past. More substantial creatures, deer, amble across the path from time to time, secure in their well-being. There are few lovelier places to stroll and dream than at Wormsloe.

Blackberry Cake with Seven-Minute Frosting

This is a much-requested cake that I make only when blackberries are in season.

Frosting

2 egg whites

1 1/2 cups sugar

5 tablespoons water

1 1/2 teaspoons light corn syrup

1 teaspoon vanilla extract

Blackberry Cake

1 3/4 cups fresh blackberries

2 cups sugar

1 cup shortening, at room temperature

3 eggs, beaten

3 cups all-purpose flour

1 teaspoon baking soda

1/2 teaspoon salt

1 teaspoon ground cloves

1 teaspoon ground allspice

1 teaspoon ground nutmeg

1 cup buttermilk, at room temperature

To prepare the frosting, combine the egg whites, sugar, water, and corn syrup in the top of a double boiler and mix until the sugar is dissolved. Pour boiling water into the bottom of the double boiler and beat constantly with an egg beater for 7 minutes, until the frosting will stand in peaks. Remove from the heat. Add the vanilla extract, and continue to beat with a spoon until the frosting is thick enough to spread, 2 to 3 minutes.

Preheat the oven to 350°. Lightly grease 3 (8-inch) round cake pans with nonstick cooking spray and lightly flour, tapping the excess flour out.

To prepare the cake, in a saucepan, boil 1 cup of water over high heat. Turn off the heat, drop the blackberries in, and drain immediately. With an electric mixer on medium speed, cream together the sugar and shortening. Add the eggs and mix well. Sift the flour, baking soda, salt, cloves, allspice, and nutmeg together and add to the egg mixture in batches, alternating with the buttermilk and mixing each batch in well. Fold in the berries. Divide the batter among the cake pans. Bake for

30 minutes, until an inserted toothpick comes out clean. Let cool for 10 to 15 minutes on wire racks before inverting out of the pans and allowing to cool completely. Place 1 layer on a serving platter and frost with one-third of the frosting. Place another cake layer on top, frost with another one-third of the frosting. Top with the last cake layer and frost with the remaining frosting.

Sangria

Serve this with a caveat to your guests; it is one potent potable!

¹/₂ cup sugar
4 lemons, cut into ¹/₄-inch slices
4 oranges, cut into ¹/₄-inch slices
2 Red Delicious apples, cut into wedges
4 cups dry red wine
¹/₄ cup brandy or rum
3 cups ginger ale
2 bananas, diced

In a large pitcher, combine the sugar, lemons, oranges, and apples, and stir well. Add the wine and rum and refrigerate for 4 to 5 hours or overnight. Just before serving, stir in the ginger ale and bananas. Serve cold in glass pitchers or in your favorite punch bowl.

Ladies' Bridge Club Luncheon

Serves 4

❦

"I both love and hate catering the bridge clubs. I love the ladies and enjoy their lively company, but it's very tricky to do these things right."

❦

Tomatoes Provençal

Shrimp Oriental in Bread Baskets

Cold Asparagus Wrapped in a Lemon Ring and Served with Vinaigrette

Fruit Compote with Grand Marnier Sauce

❦

I am trying to believe that I know more of the social life of Savannah than the facts justify. One of the things I have heard is that receptions for ladies, especially young ladies, are often given in the forenoon, and are followed by lunches which do not prevent the ladies from going home to dinner at two o'clock, with supper at seven, when the gentlemen of their families come from business to join them.

—WILLIAM DEAN HOWELLS, *SAVANNAH TWICE VISITED* (1919)

In a city known for its social clubs, there is none more exclusive than the Married Woman's Card Club, also called simply Married Woman's. Founded in 1893 by sixteen women, there remain today sixteen members who meet once a month on a Tuesday for several hours of card playing, cocktails, loud chatter that escalates with each round of drinks, and, most important, a light lunch or dinner provided by one of Savannah's premier caterers.

Guests—no fewer than thirty-two and no more than forty-eight—are invited at the discretion of the hostess and only by engraved invitation. Ladies arrive shortly before the appointed hour, which is 11:30 A.M. or 4:00 P.M. before Lent, 4:30 after Lent, or 7:30 in the evening. The evening hour includes men, who must wear formal attire. The ladies, who are always dressed to kill, wait outside in a cheerful group until the doors are opened and they are welcomed inside by their hostess and her servers. To be a hostess for Married Woman's is to watch the clock, for there is a set order to the proceedings, which always includes three rounds of drinks. At the appointed time, linens and silver are passed out, card playing ceases, and luncheon, supper, or dinner is served. The menu is typically tied to a theme of the hostess's choice, and often includes Savannah's favorite seafood: shrimp.

A singular Savannah institution, the Married Woman's Card Club is the exclusive domain of Old Savannah bloodlines, where membership is in the breeding. To cater a Married Woman's Card Club is to clock-watch—it's all in the timing, which has not altered since the first ladies gathered, gloves stowed in pocketbooks, cards fanned in fingers:

5:00 *Bridge commences; ice water is poured.*
5:30 *First drinks are poured, hors d'oeuvres are passed.*
5:45 *Second drinks are poured, hors d'oeuvres are passed.*
6:00 *Third drinks are poured, hors d'oeuvres are passed.*
6:15 *Dinner is served.*
7:00 *Married Woman's Card Club is adjourned.*

Perhaps the Married Woman's Card Club was formed as a sly response to the men's many social assemblies that excluded women, formal groups such as the Madeira Society or Rotary Club, and informal gatherings around poker tables or bar counters. One can imagine that, despite the white gloves and careful manners, the ladies must have had some fun—especially after six!

Tomatoes Provençal

I have eaten tomatoes Provençal all over France, and my recipe stands up to the best of them.

4 or 5 cloves garlic, minced
4 tablespoons fresh parsley, chopped
$^{1}/_{4}$ teaspoon dried thyme
$^{1}/_{4}$ teaspoon freshly ground black pepper
$^{1}/_{2}$ teaspoon salt
$^{1}/_{2}$ cup extra virgin olive oil
1 cup unseasoned fresh bread crumbs
4 large, ripe tomatoes

Preheat the oven to 400°. In a bowl, combine all the ingredients except the tomatoes. Cut the tomatoes in half and hollow out the seeds and pulp with a small spoon. Fill the spaces with the stuffing and place in a baking dish. Bake for 20 minutes, until warm throughout.

Shrimp Oriental in Bread Baskets

The shrimp is also delicious over Chinese noodles or rice.

Bread Baskets

1 loaf white sandwich bread, unsliced
8 tablespoons unsalted butter, melted

$^{1}/_{2}$ cup unsalted butter
1 small onion, chopped
7 tablespoons all-purpose flour
2 cups milk
3 stalks celery, chopped
1 (16-ounce) can mixed Asian vegetables (such as water chestnuts,
    bamboo shoots, bean sprouts), drained
1$^{1}/_{2}$ teaspoons soy sauce
Salt
Freshly ground black pepper
2 cups large shrimp (31 to 35 count), peeled, deveined, and tails removed

To prepare the bread baskets, preheat the oven to 250°. Slice the loaf into four equal pieces. Hollow out the center of each piece, leaving a 1-inch border of bread and a bottom. Brush with the melted butter inside and outside, and bake for about 15 minutes, until crisp and toasted light brown. Set the bread baskets aside while you prepare the shrimp.

To prepare the shrimp, preheat the oven to 375°. In a skillet, melt the butter over medium-high heat. Add the onion and sauté for about 8 minutes, until transparent. Add the flour and blend in with a whisk. Gradually add the milk, whisking constantly until the mixture is smooth and thick. Add the celery, mixed vegetables, and soy sauce, and season to taste with salt and pepper.

Meanwhile, bring a large pot of salted water to a boil. Drop in the shrimp and cook them just until they turn pink, 2 to 3 minutes. Drain the shrimp and add to the skillet with the other ingredients. Transfer to a 9 by 13-inch casserole and bake for 25 to 30 minutes, until warm throughout.

To serve, spoon one-fourth of the shrimp mixture into each bread basket and serve immediately.

Cold Asparagus Wrapped in a Lemon Ring and Served with Vinaigrette

Asparagus is a particularly popular spring vegetable in Savannah. Be careful not to overcook it; asparagus should be just fork tender.

Vinaigrette

1 cup balsamic vinegar
7 tablespoons Dijon mustard
6 level tablespoons firmly packed brown sugar
1 cup olive oil
1 cup vegetable oil

1½ pounds fresh asparagus, trimmed
1 lemon

To prepare the vinaigrette, combine the vinegar, mustard, and sugar in a food processor and process until well blended. With the motor still running, slowly add the oils until well blended.

Bring a deep saucepan full of enough water to cover asparagus to a rapid boil over high heat. Add the asparagus and boil for 2 minutes. Drain, then immerse in ice or cold water to halt the cooking, and drain again. Slice the lemon into 5 rounds and cut out the cores. Push 5 or 6 asparagus spears through each round of lemon to make individual servings. Place the asparagus bundles on a serving platter and drizzle with the vinaigrette.

Asparagus is an ancient food, cultivated by Greeks and Romans as early as 200 B.C. A welcome harbinger of spring and a part of many Easter dinners, asparagus was enthusiastically harvested at Monticello and remains a favorite on Southern tables. Some may be surprised to learn that the subtle-tasting asparagus is related to onions, garlic, and other plants in the lily family. There are three main types of asparagus—green, white, and purple—and there are many varieties within these.

Fruit Compote with Grand Marnier Sauce

Fruit for dessert is always refreshing. Here the fruits' flavors are enhanced by the addition of an elegant sauce that makes even the simplest luncheon an occasion.

Grand Marnier Sauce

5 egg yolks, at room temperature

³/₄ cup plus 1 tablespoon sugar

¹/₄ cup Grand Marnier

1 cup heavy cream

1 pint blackberries

1 pint strawberries

1 pint raspberries

To prepare the sauce, in the top of a double boiler, beat the egg yolks with a whisk until light yellow. Whisk in the ³/₄ cup sugar and put over simmering water. Continue to whisk and cook until thick, about 20 minutes. Remove from the heat and whisk until cool. Stir in the Grand Marnier.

With an electric mixer on medium speed, beat the cream in a bowl until thickened but still pourable. Add the 1 tablespoon sugar and stir to mix. Stir into the Grand Marnier sauce, cover, and refrigerate overnight.

Divide the sauce among 4 dessert bowls, spoon on the fruit, and serve.

Chef Joe Randall's
Sunday Brunch

Serves 8

❧

"Everything I cook has been shaped by hundreds of hands before me. I owe my success to all those cooks—mainly black and white women— who figured out what's good in the first place."

❧

Creamy Stone-Ground Grits with Sea Island Smothered Shrimp

Salmon Cakes

Southern Fried Catfish Fillets

Grilled Quail

Country Dinner Rolls

Cheddar Cheese Biscuits

Savannah Pecan Rolls with Sticky Topping

❧

Their food, instead of bread, is flour of Indian corn boiled, and seasoned like hasty-pudding; and this is called homminy.

—JAMES OGLETHORPE ON SAVANNAH'S NATIVE AMERICANS (1733)

Sunday in Savannah—and in fact, throughout the South—means going to church, whether one attends services in one of the magnificent downtown churches, in a new suburban structure, or in one of the casual island congregations, where khakis and golf shirts are acceptable attire for those parishioners eager to hit the rivers or the links right after early services. What is important is that you attend church *somewhere*: the subject is considered perfectly acceptable to broach for Savannahians who are sizing up newcomers.

Savannah is proud of its religious history. John Wesley, the father of Methodism, preached at Christ Church while he lived briefly in Savannah. The third Jewish congregation in America was organized in Savannah in 1733, and descendants of the first members erected the Gothic-style Mickve Israel Temple in 1878. Both the First African Baptist Church and the First Bryan Baptist Church, two of the oldest black congregations in the United States, were organized in the late 1700s. Tourists often include sanctuaries on their lists of places to visit. Typically guests visit the stunning Cathedral of St. John the Baptist, St. John's Episcopal Church, Independent Presbyterian Church, and St. Paul's Greek Orthodox Church before driving to the Isle of Hope to walk the grounds of the Isle of Hope United Methodist Church, which features a white frame sanctuary and a graveyard filled with Confederate soldiers.

Church is followed by Sunday lunch or brunch, particularly in the event of some special religious occasion—baby christening, youth confirmation, or new-member celebration. Feeding the soul can make a body hungry, and this Sunday brunch presented by Chef Joe Randall is a meal to satisfy any appetite.

Creamy Stone-Ground Grits with Sea Island Smothered Shrimp

The abundant shellfish—oysters, shrimp, and crab—along the coastal islands of Georgia provide the substance for this dish, which was created by African Americans who lived along the barrier islands, including Sapelo and St. Simons.

Shrimp Stock
Makes 3 cups

2 tablespoons peanut oil

³/4 pound shrimp shells

I celery stalk, coarsely chopped

I small carrot, coarsely chopped

I small onion, coarsely chopped

2 cloves garlic, chopped

I quart water

2 tablespoons dry white wine

I tablespoon tomato paste

I sprig parsley

I sprig thyme

2 black peppercorns

I bay leaf

Creamy Stone-Ground Grits

3¹/2 cups water

¹/2 teaspoon salt

¹/4 teaspoon freshly ground white pepper

I cup stone-ground yellow grits

I tablespoon salted butter

¹/2 cup heavy cream

Smothered Shrimp

2 pounds medium shrimp (35 to 40 count), peeled, deveined, and tails removed

I cup all-purpose flour

4 slices bacon, diced

I Vidalia onion, diced

4 cloves garlic, minced

I tablespoon paprika

(continued)

9 fresh chives, chopped

3 scallions, thinly sliced, white part and some of green

$^1/_2$ teaspoon cayenne pepper

Salt

Freshly ground black pepper

To prepare the stock, heat the oil in a stockpot over medium heat. Add the shrimp shells and sauté for 3 to 4 minutes, stirring, until the shells look dry. Add the celery, carrot, onion, and garlic, and continue to sauté for 2 to 3 minutes. Add the water, wine, tomato paste, parsley, thyme, peppercorns, and bay leaf. Bring to a boil over medium-high heat, then decrease the heat to medium, cover, and simmer for 1 hour. Strain through a fine-meshed sieve and return to the heat. Boil over medium-high heat for 10 to 20 minutes, or until reduced to 3 cups.

To prepare the grits, bring the water to a boil in a large saucepan. Add the salt and pepper and gradually stir in the grits. Cook over low heat, covered, for 20 to 25 minutes, stirring frequently, until all the water has been absorbed. Remove from the heat and stir in the butter and then the cream. Cover and set aside.

To prepare the smothered shrimp, rinse the shrimp and pat dry with paper towels. Dredge the shrimp in the flour, shaking off the excess. In a large skillet over medium-high heat, fry the bacon for 2 to 3 minutes, until brown. Add the onion and sauté for 2 minutes. Add the garlic and paprika, stir, then add the shrimp. Cook for 3 minutes, until the shrimp turn pink. Add the stock and chives and stir. Decrease the heat to medium-low and simmer, covered, for 10 minutes. Add the scallions and cayenne pepper, stir, and season with salt and pepper.

Spoon the grits into the center of 8 warm soup plates, then spoon the smothered shrimp over the grits. Serve immediately.

"Boiled hominy and butter for breakfast as an accompaniment to shrimp, or sausages or bacon, according to the season, and a plate piled high with white fluffy rice for dinner, is as regular a thing in this part of the world as is wine with your meals in France."

—Harriet Ross Colquitt,
***Savannah Cookbook* (1933)**

Salmon Cakes

Canned fish is a staple that's been used historically throughout the South. It is easily stored and quickly prepared, making it a wonderful component for breakfast, lunch, or a light supper.

2 cups plus 2 tablespoons unsalted butter
2 (10-ounce) cans pink salmon, drained
1 onion, minced
$^1/_2$ large green bell pepper, seeded, deribbed, and minced
2 egg yolks
2 teaspoons whole-grain mustard
1 cup mayonnaise
1 teaspoon freshly squeezed lemon juice
1 teaspoon Worcestershire sauce
1 tablespoon chopped fresh dill
1 teaspoon celery salt
$^1/_2$ teaspoon salt
$^1/_2$ teaspoon freshly ground black pepper
$^1/_8$ teaspoon cayenne pepper
1 cup Club Cracker crumbs
$^1/_2$ cup all-purpose flour

Clarify the 2 cups of butter by slowly melting it in a skillet over low heat until the liquids and solids dissolve and separate. Skim off any foam. Pour into a glass container and refrigerate until the butter is solid. Discard the liquid that will have sunk to the bottom of the container. The remaining solid (about 1$^1/_2$ cups) has a higher smoking point and so is better for high-heat cooking.

Remove the bones and skin from the salmon. Using a fork, flake the salmon and set aside. In a small sauté pan or skillet, melt the remaining 2 tablespoons whole butter over medium-high heat. Add the onion and green pepper and sauté for 2 to 3 minutes, until tender. Transfer to a bowl and let cool slightly. Add the egg yolks, and beat with a wire whisk until incorporated. Whisk in the mustard, mayonnaise, lemon juice, Worcestershire sauce, dill, celery salt, salt, black and cayenne peppers, and cracker crumbs. Mix well. Add the salmon and continue to stir until mixed well. Using a $^1/_3$ cup measure, form into 16 (2-inch) patties. Dust the cakes with the flour.

Heat one-fourth of the clarified butter in a skillet over medium-high heat until a wooden spoon inserted in the center causes bubbles to form. Fry the cakes in batches for 4 to 5 minutes on each side, adding butter as necessary, until golden brown. Serve hot.

Southern Fried Catfish Fillets

Catfish is a staple of Southern cuisine; its flesh is sweet, tender, and flaky, and it's wonderful when breaded with seasoned cornmeal, and fried to perfection. Serve it with tartar sauce or hot sauce.

3 pounds catfish fillets, patted dry
1 cup peanut oil
1 cup fine yellow cornmeal
1 teaspoon salt
1 teaspoon freshly ground black pepper

Cut the fillets into 3- to 4-ounce pieces. Heat the oil in a large cast-iron skillet over medium-high heat until a wooden spoon inserted in the center causes bubbles to form. In a small bowl, combine the cornmeal, salt, and pepper. Dredge the fish in the seasoned cornmeal. Fry in the hot oil until golden brown on one side, 3 to 5 minutes, then turn and cook on the other side until done, about 3 minutes longer. Drain on paper towels and serve immediately.

Catfish have nine lives, or so the saying should be in the South. Once scorned as a lowly "bottom-feeder," the whiskered fish slowly began to gain acceptance as its sweet, tender meat and cooking versatility were discovered. Georgia and South Carolina, however, virtually ignored the catfish in cookbooks until the mid-twentieth century, when catfish farms were developed throughout the South and the fish's popularity grew across the country. Though catfish can be prepared like other white fish, they are traditionally fried.

Grilled Quail

Craved by huntsmen throughout the region, this uniquely flavored game bird is indigenous to the South and is a staple of Southern cooking. Great grilled, fried, or stuffed, quail is appropriate for breakfast, lunch, or dinner.

$1/2$ cup Chicken Stock *(page 74)*
2 tablespoons red currant jelly
$1/4$ teaspoon crushed red pepper flakes
8 whole boneless quail
2 tablespoons peanut oil
Salt
Freshly ground black pepper

In a small saucepan, bring the stock, jelly, and pepper flakes to a boil over medium-high heat. Decrease the heat to medium-low and continue to cook until the liquid is reduced by half, about 15 minutes. Prepare a fire in a charcoal grill, preheat a gas grill, or preheat the broiler to high. If broiling, place a broiler pan under the broiler to heat. Rub the quail with the oil, and season inside and out with salt and pepper. Grill or broil (in the preheated pan) the quail evenly on both sides, basting with the syrup, until thoroughly cooked, 4 to 5 minutes on each side. Serve immediately.

Country Dinner Rolls

Fresh hot bread is something that automatically comes out of a good Southern kitchen. There is nothing better than moist hot rolls laden with fresh creamy butter.

2 (^{1}/$_4$-ounce) envelopes active dry yeast

2 cups lukewarm water

^{1}/$_2$ cup unsalted butter, room temperature

^{1}/$_2$ cup honey

2 teaspoons salt

2 eggs

7 cups bread flour

Preheat the oven to 425°. In a small bowl, dissolve the yeast in the water. In a stand mixer on medium speed, cream together the butter, honey, salt, and eggs. Stir in the dissolved yeast. With the motor still running on medium speed, slowly add 6 cups of the flour. Mix well until all the ingredients are incorporated. Turn out onto a floured surface and knead until the dough is very elastic, adding the remaining 1 cup of flour while kneading. Let rise for 2 to 4 hours on the floured surface, then punch down. Use immediately or store in the refrigerator for 1 to 2 days.

Spray nonstick cooking spray into 24 compartments of a muffin pan or pans. Separate the dough into 72 (1-inch) balls and put 3 into each of the compartments. Alternatively, roll the dough out to ^{1}/$_4$ inch thick, cut into 24 triangles, then roll into crescents. Spray a baking sheet with nonstick spray, then place the crescents on it. Either way, bake the rolls for 15 minutes, until golden brown.

Cheddar Cheese Biscuits

Cheddar cheese adds a flavorful twist to the traditional biscuit—the quintessentially Southern bread. These make a delectable addition to any Southern meal, such as country ham, chicken, or, as here, fish.

2 cups all-purpose flour
1 tablespoon baking powder
$^1/_4$ teaspoon salt
$^3/_8$ cup shredded medium-sharp cheddar cheese
1 tablespoon salted butter, melted
1 cup milk

Preheat the oven to 425°. In a large bowl, sift together the flour, baking powder, and salt. Add the cheese. Lightly mix in the butter and about $^2/_3$ cup or slightly more of the milk, just until the ingredients are combined. Turn the dough out onto a lightly floured surface and pat or roll out to $^1/_2$ inch thick. Cut with a $1^1/_2$-inch biscuit cutter into 16 biscuits. Brush the biscuits with the remaining milk, place on a baking sheet, and bake for 12 to 15 minutes, until golden brown. Serve hot.

Savannah Pecan Rolls with Sticky Topping

A great addition to any brunch is the sweet roll. Here Georgia pecans, so abundant in the Low Country, add crunch and nutty flavor.

$^1\!/_2$ batch Country Dinner Rolls dough (*page 116*)
2 tablespoons unsalted butter, melted
$^1\!/_4$ cup firmly packed brown sugar
2 tablespoons ground cinnamon

Sticky Topping

2 tablespoons unsalted butter
$^1\!/_2$ cup firmly packed brown sugar
$^1\!/_4$ cup dark or light corn syrup
$^1\!/_2$ cup chopped pecans

Roll out the dough to a 1-inch-thick rectangle, about 6 by 10 inches. Brush with the butter, sprinkle with the sugar and cinnamon, and roll up tightly into a 6-inch-long roll. Cut into 8 slices.

To prepare the topping, melt the butter in a round 9-inch cake pan over medium heat. Add the sugar and corn syrup. Mix well until evenly combined. Sprinkle the pecans into the pan and remove from the heat. Place the dough slices on top of the nut mixture. Let rise until doubled in volume, about 2 hours.

Preheat the oven to 375°. Bake for 25 to 30 minutes, until golden brown. Cool on a rack for 5 minutes, then cover the pan with a serving plate and invert. If the rolls stick, run a knife around the edges of the pan to loosen, and try again. Serve warm or at room temperature.

Chef Joe Randall's
Courtyard Buffet

Serves 8

✥

"Savannahians enjoy large verandas, small gardens, and any courtyard or patio where they can take advantage of the gentle climate. Breakfast, lunch, and dinner are often eaten outdoors, in settings far from either a formal dining room or a casual kitchen. Local foods lend themselves to a buffet served in a quiet courtyard."

✥

Grilled Shrimp Wrapped in Country Bacon with White Bean Cakes and
Roasted Red Pepper Vinaigrette

Marinated Black-Eyed Peas with Tender Greens

Stuffed Breast of Chicken Savannah with Crabmeat and Artichoke Dressing,
Saffron Rice, and White Wine Sauce

Stuffed Sirloin of Beef with Wild Mushroom Sauce

Country Lima Beans and Okra

Oven-Roasted New Potatoes

Southern Baked Apples

✥

*Today we had the first peas from the garden and with the addition of a lit-
tle piece of bacon from Kate had a splendid dinner. I was very hungry and
it tasted good. How rich we should feel now if we had plenty of bacon—
once a despised dish. Now the greatest luxury.*

—JULIA JOHNSON FISHER (1814–1885), DIARY (1864)

Founder James Edward Oglethorpe's design for Savannah included a series
of wards and squares, with each ward of forty lots situated around a square
where people could socialize, conduct business, and gather if attacked. Today,
twenty-one of Savannah's original downtown squares have been refurbished
into walking paradises, offering residents a place to chat with neighbors, throw
down a quilt for an impromptu picnic, feed the abundant squirrels and pigeons,
read, reflect, or people-watch.

Surrounding the squares are Savannah's historic homes, most of which date
from the late 1700s to mid-1800s. Savannah's historic district is now one of the
nation's largest historic urban landmark districts, including several thousand
architecturally and historically significant buildings in a two-and-a-half square
mile radius.

Often hidden from view are walled gardens and courtyards that are attached
to many of the homes, providing homeowners intimate private settings in which
to entertain. No two gardens are alike. They reflect the preferences of their
designers—some lush with tropical greenery, others laid out formally in English
fashion, with pathways of brick or stone and edged beds with well-tended shrubs
in intricate designs.

One such courtyard belongs to the Casey House, which provides quarters
for guests who visit the Savannah College of Art and Design. Casey House is
the location for the photographs on these pages. A courtyard dinner in such a
historic setting should, of course, reflect the bounty and good taste that
Savannah has always offered to its visitors.

Grilled Shrimp Wrapped in Country Bacon with White Bean Cakes and Roasted Red Pepper Vinaigrette

White toast made from French and Italian breads is a common canvas for chefs creating new and unusual appetizers. White bean cakes are a nice change of pace. In this dish, Asian seasonings create an alluring backdrop for the shrimp.

Roasted Red Pepper Vinaigrette

2¹/₂ cups peanut oil

³/₄ cup red wine vinegar

2 tablespoons cold water

2 tablespoons fresh basil, chopped

¹/₂ cup roasted red bell peppers (*page 127*)

1 tablespoon firmly packed brown sugar

1 clove garlic, chopped

1 teaspoon salt

1 teaspoon freshly ground black pepper

24 super-jumbo whole shrimp (16 to 20 count), peeled and deveined, tails on

¹/₂ cup peanut oil

¹/₈ teaspoon dark sesame oil

2 tablespoons seasoned rice vinegar

1 clove garlic, minced

¹/₂ tablespoon chopped cilantro

12 strips smoked bacon, cut in half crosswise

8 sprigs of basil, for garnish

White Bean Cakes

1 pound dried Great Northern beans, soaked in water for 6 to 8 hours
2 quarts water
1 ham hock, split
1 sprig parsley
1 teaspoon salt
$^1/_2$ cup clarified butter (*page 112*)
1 small onion, minced
4 cloves garlic, minced
Freshly ground black pepper
$^1/_2$ cup all-purpose flour
2 egg yolks
2 tablespoons fresh sage, chopped
$^1/_2$ teaspoon cayenne pepper

To prepare the vinaigrette, combine all the ingredients in a blender or food processor and blend until smooth. Transfer to a bowl, cover, and refrigerate for at least 1 hour or up to 1 day, until ready to serve.

Place the shrimp in a large bowl. In a small bowl, combine the peanut oil, sesame oil, vinegar, garlic, and cilantro and mix well. Pour the oil mixture over the shrimp and toss to coat evenly. Cover and refrigerate for at least 8 hours or overnight.

To prepare the bean cakes, drain the beans and place in a large saucepan with the water, ham hock, parsley, and salt. Bring to a boil over medium-high heat, then decrease the heat to medium and cook for $1^1/_2$ to 2 hours, until the beans are tender. Drain and allow to cool. Discard the parsley and refrigerate the ham hock for another use.

In a skillet over medium-high heat, heat 2 tablespoons of the clarified butter. Add the onion and garlic and cook for 1 to 2 minutes, until the onion is transparent. Season with salt and pepper, add 2 tablespoons of the flour, and cook, stirring, for 3 to 4 minutes, until all the fat is absorbed. Do not brown. Remove from heat and set aside.

Purée half of the beans in a food processor or blender until somewhat smooth. Mash the remaining beans against the side of a large bowl. Add the puréed beans to the mashed beans. Stir in the onion mixture, egg yolks, sage, and cayenne pepper. Mix well.

Line a baking sheet with parchment paper. Using a $^1/_4$-cup measure, form 8 to 10 cakes $2^1/_2$ inches in diameter and $^1/_2$ inch thick, and place on the prepared baking sheet. Cover and refrigerate for at least $1^1/_2$ hours. In a large skillet over medium-high heat, heat the remaining clarified butter. Lightly dust the cakes with the remaining flour. Cook 2 to 3 minutes on each side, or until brown and heated through.

(continued)

To grill the shrimp, prepare a fire in a charcoal grill, preheat a gas grill, or preheat the broiler to high. If broiling, place a broiler pan under the broiler to heat. Remove the shrimp from the marinade and discard the marinade. Wrap each shrimp with half a strip of bacon and secure the bacon with a toothpick. Arrange the bacon-wrapped shrimp onto long wooden presoaked skewers, about 6 shrimp per skewer.

Place the skewers on the grill or in the preheated broiling pan and cook for 3 to 4 minutes on each side, or until the bacon browns and the shrimp turn pink. Remove the shrimp from the skewers.

Place a hot bean cake onto each dinner plate and drizzle the vinaigrette over it. Arrange the shrimp around the cake. Garnish with the basil. Serve immediately.

Marinated Black-Eyed Peas with Tender Greens

The earthy flavor of black-eyed peas marries well with roasted red bell peppers. An integral food of the South, black-eyed peas lend themselves to a variety of preparations—served hot either alone or with another vegetable, or cold as part of a salad.

Black-Eyed Peas with Ham Hocks

I pound fresh or dried black-eyed peas
I smoked ham hock, split
I quart water
¹/₂ small onion, chopped
³/₄ teaspoon crushed red pepper flakes
2¹/₂ teaspoons fresh thyme, chopped
¹/₂ teaspoon salt
¹/₂ teaspoon freshly ground black pepper

Marinade

1 red bell pepper
1/2 red onion, diced
2 cloves garlic, minced
2 tablespoons fresh basil, chopped
1 tablespoon fresh parsley, chopped
3/4 cup peanut oil
1/4 cup red wine vinegar
1 1/2 teaspoons firmly packed dark brown sugar
1 teaspoon Worcestershire sauce
1 teaspoon salt
1/4 teaspoon freshly ground black pepper
1/4 teaspoon crushed red pepper flakes

4 cups mesclun salad greens
1/2 cup Roasted Red Pepper Vinaigrette (*page 124*)
2 tomatoes, peeled, seeded, and finely diced
1 red onion, diced

First, prepare the black-eyed peas with ham hocks. If you're using dried peas, soak them for 6 to 8 hours in water to cover. Bring the ham hock and the 1 quart water to a boil in a saucepan over medium-high heat, making sure that the hocks are covered by the water. Decrease the heat to medium and simmer, covered, for about 45 minutes, until the meat can be easily removed from the bone. Remove the hocks from the pan, discard the skin and bone, dice the meat into small pieces, and return it to the stock. Add the peas, onion, pepper flakes, thyme, salt, and pepper. Bring to a boil over medium-high heat, then decrease the heat to medium, cover, and simmer for 30 minutes.

To prepare the marinade, first roast the red bell pepper. Put the pepper over a hot flame or under the broiler until it is charred all over. Place it in a brown paper bag, seal it, and set it aside until it is cool enough to handle, about 15 minutes. Remove the charred skin, cut the pepper in half, remove the seeds, and dice. This yields about 1 cup diced roasted pepper, depending on the size of the pepper.

Combine the roasted pepper, onion, garlic, basil, parsley, and cooked peas in a large bowl. In a small bowl, combine the oil, vinegar, sugar, Worcestershire sauce, salt, pepper, and pepper flakes. Pour over the black-eyed pea mixture, toss to coat evenly, and refrigerate overnight.

To prepare the greens, toss the mesclun greens in a bowl with the vinaigrette. Arrange in the center of 8 chilled salad plates. Top with the peas, tomatoes, and diced red onion. Serve immediately.

Stuffed Breast of Chicken Savannah with Crabmeat and Artichoke Dressing, Saffron Rice, and White Wine Sauce

This is an elegant way to prepare and serve chicken; the delicate flavor of the crabmeat enhances that of the tender artichoke, culminating in an exceptional dish.

Crabmeat and Artichoke Dressing

2 tablespoons salted butter

1 small onion, minced

2 egg yolks

1 teaspoon dried mustard

4 slices white bread, crusts removed, flattened, and finely diced

$^1/_8$ teaspoon cayenne pepper

1 teaspoon seafood seasoning

$^1/_4$ cup mayonnaise

1 tablespoon fresh parsley, chopped

4 dashes Tabasco sauce

1 teaspoon Worcestershire sauce

$^1/_2$ teaspoon freshly squeezed lemon juice

$^1/_2$ teaspoon salt

$^1/_2$ teaspoon freshly ground white pepper

1 pound lump crabmeat, picked clean for shell

1 (14$^1/_2$-ounce) can artichoke bottoms, drained and diced

8 chicken breasts, skin on

1 teaspoon salt

1 teaspoon freshly ground black pepper

2 tablespoons salted butter, melted

1 teaspoon paprika

Saffron Rice

$^1/_4$ cup salted butter

2 cups long-grain white rice

4 cups Chicken Stock (*page 74*)

$^3/_4$ teaspoon saffron threads, crushed

$^1/_2$ teaspoon salt

White Wine Sauce
1 cup white wine
1 large shallot, minced
$^1/_2$ cup heavy cream
2 tablespoons salted butter
1 teaspoon paprika
Salt
Freshly ground black pepper

To prepare the dressing, melt the butter in a small sauté pan over medium heat. Add the onion and sauté for 2 to 3 minutes, until transparent. In a large bowl, combine the onion, egg yolks, and mustard and mix well. Stir in the bread, cayenne pepper, seafood seasoning, mayonnaise, parsley, Tabasco sauce, Worcestershire sauce, lemon juice, salt, and pepper. Gently fold in the crabmeat and artichoke pieces, being careful not to break up the crabmeat lumps.

To prepare the chicken, preheat the oven to 350°. Cut a 2-inch pocket in the side of each chicken breast. Place 2 tablespoons of the dressing in each pocket. Season each chicken breast with salt and pepper and place in a roasting pan, skin side up. Brush with the melted butter, sprinkle with paprika, and bake for 20 to 30 minutes, until golden.

To prepare the rice, melt the butter in a saucepan over medium-high heat. Add the rice and cook, stirring to coat the rice well with butter, about 1 minute. Stir in the stock, saffron, and salt. Bring to a boil, cover, then decrease the heat to medium-low and simmer undisturbed for 20 minutes, until the rice is tender and all the stock is absorbed.

To prepare the sauce, heat the wine in a saucepan over high heat and add the shallot. Bring to a boil, and boil until reduced by half, about 10 minutes. Turn off the heat and add the cream. Whisk until smooth. Whisk in the butter, then the paprika, and season with salt and pepper. Keep warm until serving.

To serve, place a bed of the rice on each of 8 heated dinner plates. Slice the chicken on the bias into 2-inch slices, arrange the slices on the rice, and ladle the sauce over.

Stuffed Sirloin of Beef with Wild Mushroom Sauce

This is a wonderful way to use the ends of a sirloin strip, which may not be tender.

Brown Veal Stock
Makes 1 quart

3 pounds veal bones

1/2 onion, coarsely chopped

2 small carrots, coarsely chopped

2 stalks celery, coarsely chopped

1 leek, white part only, coarsely chopped

2 quarts water

1 cup canned whole peeled tomatoes, chopped

1 bay leaf

1 sprig parsley

4 whole black peppercorns

2 teaspoons salt

Wild Mushroom Sauce

2 tablespoons salted butter

1 large shallot, minced

1/4 pound porcini mushrooms, sliced

1/4 pound chanterelle mushrooms, sliced

1/2 pound cremini mushrooms, sliced

Salt

Freshly ground black pepper

2 tablespoons all-purpose flour

1/4 cup dry sherry

1 tablespoon fresh parsley, chopped

8 (8-ounce) slices sirloin steak, trimmed

Stuffing

1 tablespoon salted butter

2 large shallots, minced

3 cloves garlic, minced

1 pound cremini mushrooms, finely diced

2 teaspoons fresh tarragon, chopped

2 cups unseasoned fresh bread crumbs

Salt

Freshly ground black pepper

8 slices country bacon

To prepare the stock, preheat the oven to 400°. In a roasting pan, roast the veal bones for 1 hour, turning at 30 minutes. Add the onion, carrots, celery, leek, and continue roasting until the vegetables are brown, about 30 minutes. Remove the pan from the oven and put the bones in a stockpot. Drain the vegetables and add them to the pot, discarding the pan juices. Add the water (it should cover the bones and vegetables), then add the tomatoes, bay leaf, parsley, peppercorns, and salt. Bring to a boil, decrease the heat to low, and simmer, covered, for 7 to 8 hours. Strain through a fine-meshed sieve and allow to cool. Leftover stock can be kept up to 3 days in the refrigerator, or it can be frozen.

To prepare the sauce, melt the butter in a saucepan over medium-high heat. Add the shallot and sauté for 1 minute, until tender. Add all the mushrooms, season with salt and pepper, and sauté for 3 to 4 minutes, until soft. Stir in the flour, then 2 cups of the stock. Bring to a boil, decrease the heat to medium-low, and simmer, covered, for 30 minutes. Stir in the sherry and parsley. Adjust seasoning with salt and pepper if necessary and simmer for 4 to 5 minutes more. Keep warm while you prepare the meat.

Place 1 slice of steak between 2 pieces of plastic wrap. With a cleaver or mallet, flatten the slice evenly to $1/4$ inch thick. Set aside, and repeat with remaining steak slices.

To prepare the stuffing, preheat the broiler and preheat the oven to 350°. In a skillet, melt the butter over medium-high heat. Add the shallots and garlic and sauté for 1 minute, until tender. Add the mushrooms and continue to sauté for 4 to 5 minutes, until soft. Add the tarragon and bread crumbs, stir, and remove from the heat. Stir in $1/2$ cup of the stock, season with salt and pepper, and mix well.

With the steak slices laid out flat, spoon $1^1/2$ tablespoons of the stuffing over each. Roll tightly and wrap each with a slice of bacon. Place in a baking dish and broil for 2 to 3 minutes per side, until the bacon is crisp. Transfer the dish to the oven and cook for 3 to 4 minutes, until the meat is brown. Remove from the oven, allow to cool slightly, and slice each stuffed steak on the diagonal into 3 pieces.

To serve, spoon the sauce onto 8 heated dinner plates and arrange the sliced steak on top. Serve hot.

Country Lima Beans and Okra

Lima beans fresh from the garden are a traditional part of rural Southern cuisine and culture. Here the beans are infused with the flavor of the tender okra.

3 tablespoons salted butter

1 onion, finely diced

1 green bell pepper, seeded, deribbed, and finely diced

2 cups water

2 cups frozen large lima beans

2 teaspoons sugar

1 cup small okra pods

$^1/_2$ teaspoon salt

$^1/_4$ teaspoon freshly ground black pepper

1 teaspoon cayenne pepper

In a large skillet, melt 2 tablespoons of the butter over medium-high heat. Add the onion and bell pepper and sauté for 2 to 3 minutes, until the onion is transparent and the pepper is tender. Pour in the water and add the lima beans. Bring to a boil, then decrease the heat to medium, add the sugar, and simmer for 10 to 12 minutes, until the lima beans are tender.

Lima beans were named for their discovery in Lima, Peru by early European settlers. Though not an exclusively Southern crop, they are the most popular bean in many parts of the South, where they are better known as "butter beans" for their rich, creamy texture. Limas are a shell bean and must be shucked from their hard pod when fresh—a task well worth the resulting flavor.

Over medium-high heat, bring a small saucepan full of water to a boil. Drop in the okra and blanch for 45 seconds. Drain, plunge into ice water to halt cooking, and drain again. Add the okra to the onion, pepper, and lima bean mixture and continue to cook for 3 minutes, until tender. Stir in the remaining 1 tablespoon butter, season with salt and black and cayenne peppers, and serve hot.

Oven-Roasted New Potatoes

The perfect alternative to the baked potato, this fragrant dish makes use of the fresh rosemary so abundant in the gardens of Savannah.

1/2 cup peanut oil
1 teaspoon salt
1/2 teaspoon freshly ground black pepper
1 teaspoon paprika
2 teaspoons fresh rosemary, chopped
3 pounds new red potatoes, washed and halved

Preheat the oven to 350°. Combine the oil, salt, pepper, paprika, and rosemary in a bowl and mix well. Add the potatoes and stir to coat evenly. Put the potatoes in a baking dish, cut side down. Bake for 30 minutes, turning at 15 minutes, until fork tender and brown.

Southern Baked Apples

This dish is delicate in flavor and can be prepared quickly. Serve warm with ice cream, whipped cream, crème fraîche, or plain cream.

Syrup
1/2 cup water
1 teaspoon freshly squeezed orange juice
6 tablespoons firmly packed brown sugar
4 tablespoons granulated sugar
Pinch of cinnamon
2 teaspoons freshly squeezed lemon juice
4 teaspoons grated lemon zest
1/4 teaspoon salt

8 Granny Smith apples
2 tablespoons firmly packed brown sugar, for topping

Preheat the oven to 350°. Combine all the syrup ingredients in a saucepan and bring to a boil over medium-high heat. Continue to boil until the mixture is syrupy, 3 to 5 minutes. Peel the top 2 inches of each apple. Core the apples and place them upright in a baking dish. Pour the syrup over and into the apples. Cover with aluminum foil and bake for 30 minutes. A fork will glide through the apples when they are done. Preheat the broiler. Sprinkle the apple tops with the 2 tablespoons brown sugar and broil for 3 minutes, until the sugar begins to caramelize. Serve immediately.

Specialty Dishes

Black-eyed peas, greens, and sweet potatoes are among the staples of Southern cuisine. Every cook has a favorite rendition of these country favorites. But today's nutrition- and diet-conscious chefs, and the multicultural diversity that characterizes the New South, demand alterations from the usual methods of preparing old favorites. In these specialty recipes, Savannah's chefs offer new twists guaranteed to perk up the palate and give an old favorite a new personality. Here is culinary proof that all things old can be new again.

Black-Eyed Pea Salsa
Joe Randall

Serves 8

This salsa is a wonderful alternative to the usual black-eyed pea dish served on New Year's Day. Guaranteed to bring good luck the whole year through!

Peas

1 pound black-eyed peas
1 small onion, diced
$1/4$ teaspoon crushed red pepper flakes
1 ham hock
1 quart water

$1/2$ tomato, finely diced
1 small onion, finely diced
1 green bell pepper, seeded, deribbed, and finely diced
4 stalks celery, finely diced
8 ounces ($1/2$ pound) lean smoked ham, chopped
1 cup finely diced serrano chiles
2 tablespoons extra virgin olive oil
$1/4$ teaspoon salt
$1/8$ teaspoon freshly ground black pepper
1 tablespoon fresh parsley, chopped

To prepare the peas, combine the peas, onion, pepper flakes, ham hock, and water in a stockpot and bring to a boil over medium-high heat. Cover, decrease the heat to medium, and simmer for $1^1/2$ hours, until tender. Drain and set aside. Refrigerate the hock for another use.

In a large bowl, combine the tomato, onion, bell pepper, celery, ham, chiles, and pea mixture. Stir well. In a small bowl, combine the oil, salt, black pepper, and parsley and pour over the vegetables. Mix well. Refrigerate until needed, up to 5 days. Serve cold.

Corn Pudding
Susan Mason
Serves 6 to 8

I have made this recipe with frozen corn in the winter, but I have found that it is much better with fresh summer corn.

12 to 14 ears fresh yellow corn
1/4 cup all-purpose flour
1 tablespoon sugar
1 teaspoon salt
1/4 teaspoon freshly ground black pepper
2 cups heavy cream
4 tablespoons unsalted butter, melted
3 eggs, well beaten
4 large tomatoes

Preheat the oven to 350°. Spray a 1 1/2-quart baking dish with nonstick spray. With a sharp paring knife, cut the corn kernels off the cobs. Purée half of the kernels in a blender for 4 seconds, until coarse. Combine the puréed corn with the whole kernels in a large bowl. Add the flour, sugar, salt, and pepper, and stir well. Mix in the cream, butter, and eggs. Pour into the prepared baking dish. Set the dish into another pan and fill the larger pan with hot water to a depth of 1 inch. Bake, uncovered, for 1 hour, until an inserted toothpick comes out clean. Cut the tomatoes in half horizontally and hollow out with a small spoon, leaving a 1-inch edge of fruit. Stuff 1/2 cup of the corn mixture into each tomato half and bake for 10 minutes, until heated through.

Sweet Potato Pancakes
Joe Randall

Serves 8

Southerners love sweet potatoes. This dish is light, quick, and is a perfect complement to pork or chicken.

1 pound sweet potatoes, peeled and shredded
1 small onion, finely diced
3 eggs
$1/4$ cup all-purpose flour
$1/2$ teaspoon baking powder
$1/4$ teaspoon ground nutmeg
$1/8$ teaspoon ground allspice
$1/2$ teaspoon salt
$1/4$ teaspoon freshly ground black pepper
$1/4$ cup peanut oil

Put the sweet potatoes and onion in a clean kitchen towel and twist to squeeze out as much liquid as possible. Transfer to a bowl, add the eggs, flour, baking powder, nutmeg, allspice, salt, and pepper and mix well.

Heat the oil in a heavy skillet over medium heat. Working in batches, spoon about $1/4$ cup of the mixture into the skillet to form pancakes 2 to 3 inches in diameter and $1/2$ inch thick. Cook for 2 to 3 minutes on each side, until golden brown. Drain on paper towels and serve hot.

Bluffton Oysters with Leeks and Ham
Elizabeth Terry

Serves 6

Native Eastern oysters develop their flavor from the waters they grow in. My favorite oysters come from Bluffton, South Carolina, a half-hour drive from Savannah. This recipe makes an elegant appetizer—briny oysters and a bit of salty country ham all mellowed with warm cream.

2 tablespoons unsalted butter

4 ounces country ham, minced

1/4 cup Pernod

2 tablespoons all-purpose flour

1 cup heavy cream

2 tablespoons fresh flat-leaf parsley, minced

2 pints fresh small oysters, drained well

3 whole leeks, sliced

6 slices Sweet Potato Brioche (*page 22*), toasted

2 tablespoons fresh tarragon, minced, for garnish

In a large skillet over high heat, melt the butter. Add the ham and sauté for 4 minutes, until brown. Pour in the Pernod and stir, then add the flour and whisk for 1 minute. Whisk in the cream and parsley and simmer for 5 to 6 minutes, whisking constantly, until the sauce becomes thick. The sauce may be made ahead to this point: set aside to cool, then refrigerate for up to 24 hours.

When ready to serve, rewarm the sauce over medium-low heat for about 3 minutes. Add the oysters and leeks, stir, and simmer for about 5 minutes, until the edges of the oysters begin to curl and the leeks are bright green. Spoon even amounts of the oyster mixture over the slices of brioche, sprinkle with the tarragon, and serve.

Spicy Collard Greens
Susan Mason

Serves 12

No bona fide Southern meal is complete without ample servings of greens. This spicy rendition is certain to win new fans to a favorite Southern staple.

Smoky Pork Stock
2 pounds smoked ham hocks
4$\frac{1}{2}$ quarts water

1 large bunch well-washed collard greens, stemmed and
    leaves cut into 1/2-inch ribbons
6 tablespoons olive oil
3 onions, coarsely chopped
2 or 3 large cloves garlic, minced
1$\frac{1}{2}$ teaspoons crushed red pepper flakes
Salt
Freshly ground black pepper
2 (28-ounce) cans whole peeled tomatoes, drained
6 summer squash

To prepare the stock, put the ham hocks and water into a stockpot and bring to a boil over medium heat. Cover, decrease the heat to low, and simmer for 2 hours, until the hocks are fork tender; the stock will be intensely flavored. Strain the stock and let it cool, then refrigerate for several hours. Skim off the fat before using. The ham hock may be discarded.

In a heavy stockpot, bring the stock to a boil over high heat. Add the collard greens, decrease the heat to medium, and simmer, covered, until tender, 30 to 40 minutes. Drain the greens and reserve the liquid.

Wipe out the pot. Add the oil and heat over medium heat. Add the onions and sauté until translucent, 5 to 6 minutes. Add the garlic and pepper flakes and season with salt and pepper. Cook, stirring, for 1 minute. Add the tomatoes and 3 cups of the reserved cooking liquid and simmer over low heat until the tomatoes begin to break down, about 15 minutes. Add the collard greens and cook until they are heated through, about 5 minutes.

Preheat the oven to 350°. Slice each squash in half lengthwise. Hollow out the center and fill with the greens. Place on a baking sheet and heat on the middle rack for 15 minutes. Serve hot.

Southern Shortcakes with Peaches, Whipped Cream, and Blueberry Sauce

Elizabeth Terry

Serves 8 to 10

Southerners are divided: there are those who serve pound cake or sponge cake for a shortcake and those who serve sweetened biscuits. I love sweetened biscuits with fruit, and I offer you my recipe served with peaches.

Shortcakes

$1/3$ cup granulated sugar
2 cups all-purpose flour
$2^1/2$ teaspoons baking powder
$1/2$ teaspoon salt
6 tablespoons unsalted butter, chilled and cubed
$1^1/4$ cups heavy cream
Powdered sugar, for dusting

Blueberry Sauce

1 pint fresh blueberries
$1/2$ cup granulated sugar
1 tablespoon freshly squeezed lemon juice

1 cup heavy cream
1 tablespoon firmly packed brown sugar
6 cups peeled and sliced peaches (8 to 10 peaches)

To prepare the shortcakes, preheat the oven to 350°. Cover a baking sheet with parchment paper or spray it with nonstick spray. In a bowl, combine the granulated sugar, flour, baking powder, and salt. Cut in the butter using 2 knives or a pastry cutter until the crumbs are pea size. Stir in the cream. Knead 5 to 10 times in the bowl, until the dough is very soft. Turn the dough out onto a lightly floured surface and pat out to a circle 9 inches in diameter and $1/2$ inch thick. Cut with a $3^1/2$-inch biscuit cutter; be sure not to twist the cutter as you cut—this will make the shortcakes rise unevenly when they bake. You will have 8 to 10. Place on the prepared baking sheet and bake for 10 to 15 minutes, until very light brown. Remove from the oven and dust with the powdered sugar.

To prepare the sauce, combine the berries and granulated sugar in a small saucepan over medium-high heat. Bring to a boil and stir frequently for about 5 minutes, until the sugar is dissolved and the berries begin to soften. Allow to cool, add the lemon juice, and press through a fine-meshed sieve to remove most of the skin. Set aside.

In a bowl, combine the cream and brown sugar and whip with an electric mixer on high speed until stiff peaks form. Split the shortcakes in half horizontally. Place the bottom halves on dessert plates. Top each with some whipped cream and about ³/₄ cup sliced peaches, drizzle with the sauce, then cover with the shortcake top. Garnish the plates with the remaining sauce and whipped cream.

Brunch Grits
George Spriggs

Serves 6 to 8

Grits are a regular part of breakfast in Savannah; here is a creamier, more flavorful version using yellow polenta and Parmesan cheese.

3 tablespoons unsalted butter
2 large shallots, minced
2 large cloves garlic, minced
2 cups Chicken Stock (*page 74*)
1 1/2 cups half-and-half
1 cup heavy cream
1/2 cup medium-grain yellow polenta
1/4 cup freshly grated Parmesan cheese
Salt
Freshly ground black pepper

In a heavy sauté pan, melt the butter over high heat. Add the shallots and garlic and sauté until the shallots become translucent. Add the stock, half-and-half, and cream and bring to a simmer. Whisking constantly, add the polenta in a steady stream. Decrease the heat to medium-low and cook for 20 minutes, whisking occasionally. Gradually add the Parmesan, season with salt and pepper, and cook for another 20 minutes, until thick and the bubbles are slow and laborious.

Index

Page numbers in italics indicate photographs.